beach
body basics

beach
body basics

Editorial consultant:
Faye Rowe

Bath · New York · Singapore · Hong Kong · Cologne · Delhi · Melbourne

First published by Parragon in 2007

Parragon
Queen Street House
4 Queen Street
Bath BA1 1HE, UK

ISBN 978-1-4075-1736-0
Printed in Malaysia

Produced by The Bridgewater Book Company Ltd

NOTES FOR THE READER
This book uses imperial, metric, and US cup measurements. Follow the same
units of measurement throughout; do not mix imperial and metric. All spoon
measurements are level: teaspoons are assumed to be 5 ml, and tablespoons are
assumed to be 15 ml. Unless otherwise stated, milk is assumed to be whole,
eggs and individual vegetables such as potatoes are medium, and pepper is
freshly ground black pepper. Recipes using raw or very lightly cooked eggs
should be avoided by infants, the elderly, pregnant women, convalescents,
and anyone suffering from an illness. The times given are an approximate
guide only.

PICTURE ACKNOWLEDGEMENTS
The publisher would like to thank the following for permission
to reproduce copyright material: Corbis 6-7, 8, 11, 20, 21, 24, 70,
72, 77, 82, 84, 87; Getty Images 4, 15, 47, 80, 90-91; istock 9 top
(repeated artwork),12, 13, 14, 16, 22, 25, 26, 29, 31, 33, 37, 38, 45,
46, 48, 71, 75, 76, 77, 78, 85, 86, 87, 89.

Contents

Introduction

Welcome to Beach Body Basics—the ultimate guide to help you to get fitter, slimmer, and more goddess-like in time for that all-important beach holiday. Four weeks of healthy eating, exercise, and pampering, and you'll be feeling great!

Be a beach babe

The idea of parading yourself around in a skimpy swimsuit may seem remarkable right now, but rest assured that, with a little bit of hard work and dedication, you can make a visible difference to your body and look great on the beach in just four weeks.

Even if you're not naturally blessed with a model-like figure—and let's face it, who do you know in real life who is?—the advice in this book will not only help you drop a few pounds, but will also inspire you to make the most of your natural body shape and god-given beauty. Best of all, it won't feel like it's a hard plan to follow, as there's no deprivation required! We believe that fad diets will fail you in the end: many women put all the weight back on (and sometimes even more) after stopping a restrictive eating plan—which is why there's no calorie or fat count given with our recipes. Strict dieting can also play havoc with your skin and hair, as it can deprive you of essential nutrients that are crucial in turning you into a true beach beauty.

Instead, we've focused on giving you suggestions for naturally healthy and nutritious meals that will help you slim while nourishing your skin and hair at the same time. Many of the pampering tips in this book use some of nature's best beauty-boosting ingredients, which are often kinder to the skin than store-bought, chemical-laden products, and much more in tune with what a true "island girl" might use. And don't worry if you're not exactly a fitness fanatic, as the exercises shown (which you'll have to do every day if you've only got four weeks to go), are easy to follow, and fun to do, too.

We want this book to be a pleasure for you to use—just think of it as your very own beach-body guru. Read it through before you begin the plan. You'll find that the advice and information is really all about helping you to make positive changes to your lifestyle so that you'll become fitter, healthier, and more radiant. Depending on how long you have to follow the plan, the changes are likely to be subtle—you'll look slimmer in your clothes, have more energy, better muscle tone, your skin will glow, and your hair will shine. You may even be able to knock a few years off your looks! If you don't want to let your friends in on your secret, you'll probably get away with saying you've been relaxing at a spa for a week. Luckily for you, this book is a lot cheaper and, we think, more fun, too!

Getting started

Ideally, you should have a full four weeks to go before you set off on your holiday. That way, you'll be much more likely to reap the rewards of following the healthy eating, fitness, beauty, and lifestyle tips in our program. But whether you've got four weeks or four months to go, you should view the advice and information on these pages as the basis for the kind of healthy lifestyle you should strive to achieve if you want to look great on the beach, all year round.

The book is divided into four sections—each designed to focus on one specific aspect of beach beauty. To help you to kick-start a new way of life, we've packed it full of healthy, delicious recipes, exercises that really work, and hair and beauty tips that'll have you glowing and gorgeous in no time. This is all brought together in the four-week planner at the end, which suggests ways of combining the tips for the ultimate all-round approach to getting the beach body you deserve.

You don't have to read all the chapters from start to finish—feel free to dip in and out of the different sections to get a feel for what's involved. We advise you to do one thing from each section every day, as laid out in the four-week planner, so you will need to read up on what recipes you'll be using on certain days to help you plan your food shopping. Similarly, you'll need to road-test each of the exercises to make sure you understand how they should be done and that you feel comfortable while you're doing them. Here's a brief outline of what's in each of the sections:

Kick-start

This section is designed to boost the effects of healthy eating, exercise, and grooming, and will get you off to a fabulous start. It provides advice on detoxing or cleansing your body, by flushing out toxins and increasing your intake of fresh fruit and vegetables. It also includes spa therapies and skin treatments. With advice on how to improve your confidence, it's your springboard to a healthier way of life.

Healthy eating

You'll love the deliciously healthy recipes and snack suggestions in this chapter. We've got 21 recipes—covering breakfast, lunch, and dinner—which use wonderful fresh ingredients such as exotic fruit, smoked chicken, and chargrilled swordfish, plus tasty vegetarian options. Each recipe is quick and easy to prepare and doesn't require any hard-to-find ingredients, so you'll have more time to spend on pampering yourself.

Getting fit

Each of the exercises in this section are designed to firm and tone trouble zones that are typically on show in a swimsuit—think thighs, buttocks, arms, and chest. They can all be carried out in the comfort of your own home and don't require any specialist equipment. We recommend you do one exercise every day and bolster the effects with regular cardiovascular work such as jogging or cycling.

Be a beach beauty

Healthy, glowing skin and glossy hair are the ultimate finishing touches to a toned figure and a confident carriage. The tips in this section, which cover everything from buffing to fake tanning, will propel you to goddess-like status and help you to feel much more confident about your looks as you stroll along the beach. Plus, pampering yourself is a great reward for sticking to the healthy eating and exercise plan, so enjoy the "me time" that this section offers.

Four-week planner

In this section, we've brought together all the different elements in the book and combined them to create a daily schedule that's both fun and effective. You may need to adapt it to suit your particular lifestyle, but you should stick to the schedule where possible, as it means you'll get the best results.

As the plan represents a healthier way of life, you can use your newfound knowledge of healthy eating and exercising to extend it, so you follow the basic principles every day of your life. After all, wouldn't it be great to look and feel fabulous 365 days a year, so you can wear a swimsuit with pride whenever you need to?

The results

We're not claiming that you will look like a supermodel overnight, but if you follow the suggestions set out in the four-week planner for a period of at least four weeks, you should start to see visible results. Not only are you likely to lose some weight, you'll also find that your muscles become more defined, making you look and feel fitter and more toned. You'll also have clearer, firmer skin and glossier hair—an excellent finishing touch to your new beach-beautiful body.

If you want to stay in your best bikini-fit shape, you should stick to the principles laid out in the book as closely as you can. Life is unpredictable and you may not be able to incorporate all the elements into your daily life. But by the time you've followed the plan for the full 28 days, it should give you enough inspiration to create healthy recipes to eat at home, to invest more time in taking care of your appearance and being active. So, what are you waiting for?

Carrying on the Plan

❋ If you have completed a full four weeks on the plan and feel so great that you want to carry it on, the best way to go about it is to draw up your own individually tailored schedule of "beach beautiful" activities that you know you will follow.

❋ Start thinking about other healthy recipes you can add to the list—and don't be afraid to experiment in the kitchen. As long as you stick to ingredients that are as fresh and wholesome as possible—rather than ready meals or convenience foods—and adopt healthy cooking methods, such as grilling, steaming, and oven baking, you can't go too far wrong. Refer to our healthy eating guidelines. Try to include as many different fruits and vegetables as you can in your diet, and opt for lean meats and fish, plus alternative vegetarian protein.

❋ Next, you need to bring in other elements, including exercise and pampering. The advice and information in this book offer you great options that you can carry on for as long as needed, but you may want to start researching new exercises with the help of a personal trainer or gym instructor. Similarly, you may be able to devise some of your own aromatherapy recipes to try. The most important thing to remember is to dedicate specific time every day to preparing healthy meals and beautifying yourself. It may be indulgent, but you'll feel and look better for it.

❋ Remember—if you plan on continuing the exercise program, you should build some rest days into your schedule so you don't end up overworking yourself, and to give your muscles some time to rest and recover.

This book will help you to...

✳ Kick-start a healthier new lifestyle.

✳ Make healthy eating more fun, with tasty and nutritious recipes to make every day.

✳ Tone up trouble zones, such as thighs, stomach, and arms, through exercise.

✳ Have glowing, gorgeous skin and hair, thanks to homemade natural lotions and potions.

✳ Plan your daily schedule, to help meet your goals.

Kick-start

Getting started is the hardest step to take. But once you've mastered the go-getting tips and advice in this section, you won't look back. There are 14 kick-start tips to choose from, ranging from quick detox treatments such as enjoying an Epsom saltbath or a facial steam, to preparing your mind with a 15-minute meditation or visualization.

Boost your beach body

These fantastic tips are designed to boost the results you'll get from healthy eating, exercise, and grooming, and put you on the fast track to bikini body status.

Let's get going

Here, you'll find a mixture of inner cleansing tips, ways to beat bloat, and insights into how to feel confident in your bikini. Choose one to do every day—see the four-week plan for guidance—and combine it with the other elements in this book for maximum effect. The extra boost you'll get from these kick-start tips will go a long way to helping you look great in time for your holiday. What's more, they're fun to do and will help you feel fantastic, too.

Many of the tips focus on getting rid of toxins from your body. This will generally help to promote a clearer skin, boost your energy levels, and improve your concentration (so you'll be more likely to stick to the plan!). There are also visualization exercises that will help you focus your mind on the goals you want to achieve. This focus is vitally important, as where the mind leads, the body often follows. If you believe in yourself and in what you can achieve, it will make the plan much easier to follow and help you to get the best results.

Say hello to Healthy Habits

To help your kick-start go as smoothly as possible, write a list of what you want to achieve to help remind you why you should stick to the plan. You might identify with some of the statements below. If your motivation takes a dip, turn to this page and read them aloud. It should be enough to get you back on track.

　❋　Having a healthier approach to life is a goal I can achieve.

　❋　Looking good on the beach will help me feel happier and more confident.

　❋　The small changes I can make now will lead to bigger rewards in the future.

　❋　Feeling great—inside and out—is something I deserve to experience.

　❋　I owe it to myself to stick to this plan and to invest time looking after my health and my looks.

Get motivated

While some of us relish the chance to make a fresh start, for others it might seem daunting. If you're suffering from last-minute nerves—it's no mean feat to change the habits of a lifetime, after all—remember that every single step you take, starting from now, can help to improve your health and well-being.

You'd be surprised at the effects that even the little things can have on the way you feel inside—not to mention the way you look on the outside. The excellent tips on how to live a more toxin-free lifestyle will help you feel great right from the beginning. You'll find that it won't take long to experience the benefits and, when you do, it will be hard to sink back into your old ways—who wouldn't rather feel healthier and more energized? Just remember all the good you'll be doing for your body and the knock-on effects that it could have on other areas of your life, from work to relationships, since when we feel better within ourselves, it often helps to improve our whole outlook. Walking along the beach in a bikini will seem much less daunting if your skin is glowing and your thoughts are cool, calm, and collected thanks to visualization and deep breathing.

Stick with it

It's not every day that we wake up feeling saintly and eager to be as healthy as possible. But if you do have a rough day, and find you don't manage to follow your routine, don't dwell on it. Simply accept it, get a good night's sleep, and start afresh tomorrow. We recommend you carry out one kick-start tip each day, preferably in the morning, to put you in a positive frame of mind for the day to follow. Soon, doing something good for your mind and body when you wake will become second nature. Now, check out our inspiring tips...

Flush away toxins

Even slim women can suffer from cellulite. In fact, around 80 percent of women in the western world have it. Cellulite can be caused by a build-up of toxins in the system: caffeine in particular, found in coffee, chocolate, and many teas and fizzy drinks, is thought to be the chief culprit.

The bumpy texture of cellulite is usually found around the thighs, buttocks, and knees, and it can get worse after having children, due to hormonal changes in the body. It's very hard to shift, and there's no cream or magic potion that can get rid of it, but experts say that if you reduce the number of toxins in your system, you can improve the look of cellulite and have a smoother, more youthful-looking silhouette.

The easiest and most natural way to cleanse and detoxify your system is to raise your water intake to around eight glasses—around $4\frac{1}{4}$ pints/ 2 liters—a day (aim for more if you are exercising a lot). Not only will this keep you hydrated and plump out your skin, but it will help the cells in your body to be more efficient, meaning they'll be better able to grow and repair themselves. The result? Cellulite should become less noticeable, your skin will be clearer and brighter, and blotchy patches will disappear. A great way to start is to drink a cup of hot water with a squeeze of lemon added to it before breakfast. Keep a pitcher of water on your desk at work if you can, to monitor your intake.

Detox with Epsom salts

Getting rid of toxins is a great way to reduce water retention. You may also find that you have a clearer skin as a result. Some experts recommend dissolving the salts in a pitcher of water and sipping it before bedtime, but the mixture does taste rather bitter. A much more enjoyable way to reap the benefits is to have an Epsom salts bath. Epsom salts are pure magnesium, which the body needs to help maintain healthy tissues, especially those in the muscles, lungs, blood vessels, and nerves. Magnesium will draw toxins from your body and improve circulation. Pour about 2lb 4oz/1kg of Epsom salts into the bath water and stir until dissolved. Relax in the bath for about five minutes, then gently massage your skin with a massage mitt for a toxin-busting boost. Epsom salts baths should be avoided if your skin is cut or grazed or you have a skin condition such as eczema.

Nourish your skin

While bathing in Epsom salts is good for detoxing, other natural ingredients, like marjoram and rosemary, can be used to nourish and tone the skin. Follow this recipe to create a skin-soothing marjoram, rosemary, and lavender milk bath:

1 Wash a generous handful of fresh marjoram and rosemary leaves and chop them up.

2 Mix them in a bowl with two tablespoons of Dead Sea mineral salts (these have a gentle detoxing effect, and are available from many health food stores and pharmacies).

3 Run the bath to a comfortable temperature, and add six tablespoons of whole milk to the water.

4 Sprinkle the salt and herb mix into the water.

5 Finally, add three drops of lavender essential oil.

6 Soak and relax for at least 20 minutes.

Refine your pores

Facial steaming has been used for centuries by beauty therapists as an effective way to deep-clean the skin's pores. It helps bring grime to the surface and expel toxins, and is great for getting rid of stubborn spots. It's ideal to steam your face just before your holiday, as having clean pores means you'll be less prone to blemishes while you're away.

1 To steam your face, pour near-boiling water into a heatproof bowl so that it is two-thirds full. If you are using a dried herb like lavender, add one teaspoon to the water; if you are using a fresh herb, add two teaspoons of freshly chopped leaves or flowers. Lean over the bowl into the steam with your head under a towel; stay there for 15 minutes.

2 When the time is up, splash your face with cool water and pat it dry—you should have a healthy pink glow. Your skin is also in the ideal state to absorb nutrients from moisturizing creams—so choose one suitable for your skin type and apply it generously.

1

2

An easy way to slim

Body wraps, which promise to shave inches off your hips and thighs by helping you to sweat out nasty toxins, can be an expensive treat in a spa. You can get the same results by doing a DIY version at home. It does require a little preparation. You need the ingredients and equipment before you begin, so stock up on plastic wrap and large towels, and clear a space in the bathroom. This recipe makes two applications of a skin-cleansing and purifying body mask.

THYME, SAGE & JUNIPER BODY MASK (MAKES TWO APPLICATIONS)

1 In a medium-size bowl put six tablespoons green clay (available from most health food stores and pharmacies) and mix in $3/4$ cup water to form a paste.

2 Add one tablespoon of olive oil (it's good for nourishing the skin) and three tablespoons of fresh thyme and sage leaves, washed and finely chopped. Stir into the paste.

3 Add six drops of juniper essential oil, then stir again, and the mask is ready to use.

HOW TO APPLY

With a damp flannel, moisten the area of skin that you want to work on. Apply the mask with your fingertips and palms, concentrating on hips, thighs, and arms. You'll have to ask a friend if you want to cover your back, too. Next, wrap the plastic wrap over the skin and lay a warm towel on top—this helps the nutrients to penetrate the skin more effectively. Relax for 20 minutes. Unwrap yourself, then thoroughly rinse off the mask in the shower. Your skin should feel tingly and look radiant. Drink plenty of water afterward to rehydrate.

TREATMENT ADVICE: Use this body mask recipe on the day of making. Avoid contact with the eyes. If the treatment gets into the eyes, rinse well with water.

Recharge, right now

Did you know that you can give your energy levels a boost simply by changing the way you stand? This simple sequence of postures can help to rest the back and ward off feelings of exhaustion, helping you get on with the plan. They are also very useful for soothing backache, migraines, and mental tension.

These postures originate from the meridian-based healing systems of the East and are commonly used as energy-balancing holds in disciplines such as shiatsu and yoga. To do them, you need to be lying down on the floor, preferably completely flat, but if this feels uncomfortable, use a folded towel to support your head. Wear comfortable loose, clothing.

1 Lying flat on your back, simply cradle the base of your skull in your hands. Feel the weight of your head, and let it rest in the support of your fingers. If you like, you can bend your legs and put your feet down flat, to help ease your back at the same time. Stay in the posture for five minutes. This posture is very helpful for migraines and neck tension.

2 Lying flat on your back with your legs out straight and your hands palm down, slide your fingers under your lower back where the S-curve of the spine leaves a gap. Your hands should be resting right at the top of your hips. This posture helps to energize the lower back; your hands should begin to feel quite warm. Stay there for five minutes. When you feel ready, push down on your hands and use your arms to help you sit up.

3 Lying flat on your back, put your right hand under the base of your skull and your left hand, palm down, at the very base of your spine. Relax, and close your eyes. After a short while, you may be able to feel the energy in your spine moving gently between both hands. This is a restful posture, which helps to ease tiredness and low energy.

3

Simple morning yoga stretches

Yoga has long been known to help reduce stress and instil a sense of inner calm into those who practice regularly. Being clear-headed and relaxed will help you achieve your goals more easily and, if you practice outside, you'll feel at one with nature too.

1

2

3

4

1 MOUNTAIN POSE: Stand with your feet shoulder-width apart, shoulders relaxed, and arms by your sides. Feel your feet firmly on the ground. Breathe deeply, and relax.

2 STANDING FORWARD BEND: Still standing, lean down slowly until your hands touch the ground. Pause, then slowly ease yourself up again. Repeat three times.

3 CAT POSE: Kneel on all fours. Relax; then, as you breathe out, arch your back, feeling the stretch all along your spine. Breathe in and release. Repeat three times.

4 CHILD POSE: From all fours, rest down on the ground with your arms and feet tucked up underneath you, in a fetal position. Breathe deeply; rest for a few minutes.

Boost your body confidence

Even women with near-perfect figures can feel nervous about stripping off on the beach. No matter how we look, we each have our own hang-ups about our body. But whatever's causing your nerves, just remember that, if you feel good, there's a high chance that you'll look good too. Sit back and think for a few minutes about the last time you were on holiday. Was there a beautiful woman languishing around the pool whose figure you envied?

Try and put your finger on exactly what it was about her that made her so attractive. Was it simply her face and figure, or the fact that she looked as if she was having a fantastic time? It may have been a combination of the two, but the chances are that at least part of what you noticed was her happy aura. When we feel relaxed and happy, our body language often mirrors our thoughts. If you think you look unattractive in your swimsuit, your shoulders might slump, you'll fidget nervously, or cross your arms across your stomach to cover up. To break free from negative thoughts, try repeating some confidence-boosting mantras in your mind, such as "I'm an attractive woman" and "I look great in my bikini." If you truly believe what you're saying, you'll find that the body will follow. You'll naturally feel better about yourself if you stand up straight, pull your stomach in toward your spine, and relax your shoulders to create a good posture (it makes you look instantly slimmer), then walk slowly and confidently. If you want to appear taller, wear a wedge heel to add extra height to your frame, and if you want to cover your buttocks, wrap a sarong around your hips—it'll be your secret security blanket. Remember, you are your own strongest critic and what flaws you do have are much more likely to be noticed by you than others, so stop fretting and start being more confident about the way you look.

Steer clear of pollutants

If living in the city has left your skin dull and dreary instead of gorgeous and glowing, it's time to start steering clear of pollutants in time for the grand unveiling. Cigarette smoke and exhaust fumes can play havoc with your complexion. Particles can settle on the skin, making it hard for it to breathe, which is why city dwellers often complain of bad skin—blemishes, blotches, and uneven tone with dry or oily patches are common complaints.

The chemicals in cigarette smoke can have just as bad an effect. Research has shown that, whether you're a smoker or are being exposed to second-hand fumes, it can age your skin by up to 20 years. This is because smoke has a drying effect on the skin's surface and restricts the blood vessels, thereby reducing the amount of blood flowing to the skin. This depletes it of oxygen and essential nutrients. Wrinkles can form and the complexion looks dull and gray—problems that even a tan won't fix.

Pollutants aren't visible to the human eye, which make them all the more difficult to avoid. But there are some simple steps you can take to reduce the number of toxic chemicals with which you come into contact. The first and most obvious step is to give up smoking. Obviously, this is easier said than done, but help is available. If you book an appointment with your physician, he or she will be able to advise you on the most effective way. If you have friends who are heavy smokers, try and ask them to stop while you spend time together. If you explain how important your new regime is to you, they'll understand.

Diet can also play a part in helping to reduce your contact with toxins. Opt for foods that are high in antioxidants, which are substances that help reduce the effect of pollutants on the skin. Fresh berries, broccoli, tomatoes, red grapes, garlic, spinach, and carrots are great choices. Pay special attention to getting more vitamin C and green tea, which are super antioxidants, into both your diet and your skincare.

Breathing techniques for calm

Breathing is something you do automatically, but it can be consciously controlled. It is well known that if you're feeling agitated, taking a deep breath will calm you down. Unfortunately, years of stress and poor lifestyle mean shallow, rapid breathing, in which we use only the top third of our lungs, but it is the norm for most of us. If you don't breathe properly, you will restrict your oxygen supply and raise your blood pressure. Correct breathing comes from the deepest area of the lungs and benefits both your body and mind. You'll benefit from a lower heart rate, reduced blood pressure, and lower levels of stress hormones. Breathing properly is essential when you're exercising—the rule is to breathe in just before you make a movement and breathe out with each effort. Remember this when it comes to doing your daily exercise.

How to breathe deeply

The following exercise, known as abdominal breathing, will help you breathe more deeply, but it can be quite difficult to master. It "accustoms" the diaphragm, the sheet of muscle forming the top of the abdomen, to help the lungs inflate and deflate without effort. You may feel a little dizzy when you start to practice—it's because you're taking in more oxygen than you're used to.

* Sit comfortably. Put one hand on your chest, the other just below the ribcage. Breathe in slowly through your nose.

* Hold the breath for a few seconds, then breathe out slowly through your mouth. Expel as much air as you can.

* Repeat three or four times. Try to concentrate solely on your breathing as you do this.

Beach and sea visualization

This technique is excellent for calming the mind; it also focuses your attention and stimulates your creative energies. As an aid to the exercise, try vaporizing a combination of essential oils in a diffuser: a mixture of two drops each of lemon, juniper, and cardamom is very uplifting. These aromas have a positive effect on mood and help to improve concentration.

Sit comfortably in an armchair, resting your hands on your lap and your head on a cushion. Dim the lights and relax. Imagine that you are walking on a long stretch of white sandy beach, which you can see curving away toward the distant horizon. The temperature is warm and there is a gentle sea breeze. The sun is shining brightly and you feel very comfortable. You walk slowly, and first you become aware of the sand beneath your toes. It is warm and silky soft to the touch, and every step you take is like a caress. Tiny grains glisten on your skin as you walk along.

You turn to look at the sea. It is quite calm and a deep aquamarine blue, shining with lighter flecks of sunlight. You gaze for a few moments at the stunning blue color, feeling it bathe your eyes. Then you walk down to the water, smelling the tang of salt, hearing the cry of seabirds and the sound of the waves. Pause for a few moments and let the scene build in your imagination; let your senses create the impressions.

Now imagine that you are going into the water, tasting the salt on your tongue and feeling the tingling, rejuvenating effect of the sea, swimming without effort, still aware of the vivid aquamarine blue color all around you. Feel how different it is to be in it as well as seeing it. Feel yourself supported by the waves, the sun still shining brightly all around you.

Now come back to the shore and, as you leave the water, feel how refreshed and revitalized you are. Take a few slow, deep breaths, flex your toes and fingers, and let your awareness come back to the room.

Meditation for a healthy mind

After dinner, at the end of a day, or after a beauty treatment, it is good to prepare for bed with a simple but very effective meditation exercise. The aim is to completely unwind your body and your mind, and you should feel very rested. Mental relaxation is as important as physical; the brain controls the chemical balance of the body, and in a relaxed state the balance changes from hyperactivity to calmness. This, in turn, benefits the heart and the whole nervous system. Meditation is simply contemplation; if you have never tried it, experiment with this exercise. The simple focus it brings will surprise you.

To get ready, wear warm, loose clothing, and perhaps a shawl around your shoulders. If you are comfortable sitting cross-legged on the floor, adopt this pose; otherwise, sit on a hard-backed dining chair with both feet on the ground and your hands resting gently in your lap. On a table in front of you, place a candle in the middle of a dinner plate. Add a few beach pebbles or fresh flowers to create a simple display. This will be your focus. Dim the lights and light the candle.

Sit comfortably and focus your gaze on the candle display. Let the soft light bathe your eyes, and look right into the flame. Candlelight is soothing to the eyes, yet in the very middle of the flame it is extremely bright; at the edges you may even see traces of blue. Each time your concentration wanders, bring it back to the flame. Be gentle with yourself the first time you do this exercise; just keep your eyes on the center.

You may begin to feel very relaxed, and conscious of your breathing or your heartbeat—this is normal, so just let it happen. Sit for about 15 minutes, continuing to focus on the flame, then stretch your fingers and toes and bring your awareness gradually back into the present.

Say goodbye to stress

Stress is something that is increasingly with us and it's all too easy to reach for food to make yourself feel better. Stress or new situations can throw the most dedicated dieter, but they don't have to sabotage your plan. The way to beat stress, and to avoid its undermining effects, is to build regular slots into your life in which you actively choose to do something to relieve it, such as going for a long walk in the country, gardening, or getting creative and painting a picture. Think of 20 things that make you feel good and build them into your life. When you feel good about yourself, you'll think and act in a more positive way. Make sure you nourish your soul, not just your body.

Stress busters

Swimming outdoors	Sculpture class
Weeding flowerbed	Choosing clothes
Seeing friends	Growing herbs
Photography	Arranging flowers
Eating al fresco	Riding bicycle
Stretching exercises	Walking dog in park

ENHANCES AND IMPROVES SMALL BUST

TIES GIVE SLIMMING EFFECT FOR SHOULDERS

TANKINI DISGUISES MIDRIFT

PADDED BIKINI ENLARGES BUST

GOOD SUPPORT FOR BUST

Buy your bikini

There's no better way to get motivated than to buy your dream bikini. Set aside a few hours this weekend to go on a shopping spree where you can concentrate on searching the rails for a great two- or one-piece to wear on the beach.

When you're out shopping, consider the colors and styles that will work best for you. If you're blond, you might consider a vivid scarlet, or choose a gentle pastel blue or pink. If you're brunette, bright white, chocolate brown, royal blue, emerald green, and lemon yellow will all look great with your coloring. If you're a redhead, opt for natural, earthy tones such as beige, brown, camel, or olive green.

Finding the right cut can make all the difference, too. If you want to lengthen your legs and slim your hips, opt for high-cut briefs. If you want your bust to appear bigger, choose padded, underwired cups or a top with a frill detail. If you want to lose inches from your stomach, look for a tankini top, which will cover this area, or stick to one solid block of color to smooth out your silhouette.

Once you've found your perfect bikini or swimsuit, hang it up on the outside of your closet. That way, every time you go to bed or wake up, you'll see your gorgeous swimsuit and it will inspire you to stick to the plan.

DEEP CUT DISGUISES LARGE THIGHS

STRING TIES MAKE LEGS APPEAR LONGER

HIGHER CUT FLATTENS STOMACH AND LIFTS BUTTOCKS

SKIRT DISGUISES LARGER BODY

SHORTS FOR BEING ACTIVE ON BEACH

Healthy eating

The recipes in this chapter are delicious, filling, and easy to make. They are not only designed to help you lose weight, but also to give you all the nutrients you need to have a glowing skin, bright eyes, and luscious locks. Cutting down on toxins, ridding yourself of water retention, and increasing your energy levels are just as important as shedding a little weight.

Eat your way to beauty

Here's how to eat your way to a bikini body without falling prey to hunger pangs. Treat yourself like a machine—you need the best fuel to run as well as you can.

Eat yourself fit

There's far more to eating healthily than losing weight. While losing a few extra pounds might be relatively high on your list of priorities, it would be unwise and possibly damaging to your looks to try to fast-track yourself to skinny status. The aim of this chapter is not only to help you lose unwanted pounds and slim down for your holiday at a sensible pace, but also to make sure you are getting all the vitamins and minerals you need for healthy, glowing skin and glossy hair. Food, after all, is fuel for the body, so it's important to put the good stuff in if we want it to show on the outside.

Getting the right amount of nutrients by eating a balanced diet is the best way forward when it comes to healthy eating. All the recipes in this chapter are relatively low in fat and calories but, as everyone's body shape and metabolism are different, we don't believe in simply eating by numbers. Instead, we've carefully chosen 21 tasty breakfast, lunch, and dinner recipes that will help you cut down on toxins, get rid of water retention, and provide your body with essential vitamins and minerals—while satisfying your taste buds. And we've included guidelines on "healthy extras" that you can have as treats from time to time, or when your body is telling you it needs an extra boost to get you through the day.

On the menu

The recipes in this book should provide inspiration for the kinds of foods you should be eating every single day of your life. You don't—and shouldn't—need to starve yourself in order to get a great figure. Eating should be enjoyable and a treat for the senses so, with that in mind, nothing is out of bounds. That's not a licence to head straight for the cookie jar, though!

You should always aim to choose your food sensibly. Cutting down on convenience foods and opting for home-cooked meals made with pure, fresh ingredients will do wonders for your health and your looks. Many people lose weight by making these simple changes to their diet, while others may find that niggling health complaints, such as feeling tired all the time or problem skin, gradually improve—that's got to be better than the results you'll get from following a fad diet. Remember, too, that if you lose weight too quickly by severely limiting your calorie and fat intake, you're more likely to pile on the pounds you lost when you start eating properly again.

The recipes in this section are so delicious, you won't even feel as though you're dieting. And they're packed with healthy, nutritious ingredients to give you enough energy to carry on your daily life without any of the irritating side effects, such as mood swings, fatigue, or lack of concentration, which can often go hand in hand with dieting. Obviously, you will need to exercise some self-control and will power if you are going to stick to the beach beautiful plan. Thinking about how you want to look in your bikini should provide enough motivation. The only thing we require you to cut out completely is alcohol, as it's full of sugar and empty calories. Excluding it from your diet is often the quickest and easiest route to a slimmer you. While it might be tough at times, the end result will definitely be worth it. Just think how proud you'll be of yourself when you finally slip into your swimsuit and head out to the beach.

Ultimately, you have to listen to your body. If you're having a particularly stressful or active day, and you feel you need an extra boost, then you should make yourself a slightly bigger portion—and don't worry about it.

Also before you start any diet, speak to your physician to make sure it doesn't conflict with any medication you are currently taking, or any pre-existing medical conditions.

Daily allowances

Everyone is different and therefore has unique nutritional needs, but there are some basic foods and liquids you should aim to include in your daily diet. Aim to ensure that the breakfast, lunch, and dinner recipes that make up your daily plan offer all of these elements, and adapt your menu plan slightly if necessary.

✳ At least $4\frac{1}{2}$ pints/2 liters of water a day (around eight glasses). You can add a bit of flavor to your water with diluted fruit juice—just make sure it's got no added sugar.

✳ At least five portions of fruit and vegetables per day, so if your recipes for the day leave you lacking, you should supplement with any type of fruit or veg that appeals to you, from apples to zucchini.

✳ If you want to do a more thorough detox, you should cut down on tea, coffee, red meat, and processed foods. Stick to the plan; and to give your digestion a rest, do not eat too much.

✳ At least five portions of bread, other cereals, and potatoes, ideally included in your main meals. Choose from breakfast cereals, pasta, rice, noodles, oats, bread (opt for wholewheat), and potatoes (try sweet potatoes, which have a high fiber content). Despite common belief, carbs don't cause weight gain—it's usually what's added to your plate of pasta (for instance, creamy cheese sauce) that's to blame. So keep your carbs as plain as possible when they're not included in the recipes, and you won't pile on the weight.

✳ Two to three servings of milk and dairy foods such as cheese and yogurt, but not butter, eggs, or cream. Serving size varies according to what you have: one serving of milk is 7 fl oz/200ml; one serving of yogurt is $5\frac{1}{2}$ oz/150 g and one serving of cheese is 1 oz/30 g. Opt for lowfat options where possible and don't be tempted to overindulge.

✳ Two to three servings of meat, fish, and alternatives. Choose lowfat versions and trim off any visible fat if you are trying to achieve a noticeable weight loss. You can choose from eggs, poultry, and meat and fish products such as beefburgers and fishcakes. Alternative non-meat sources of protein include nuts (but don't eat more than a small handful a day, as nuts are usually high in calories), tofu, textured vegetable protein, and kidney beans.

✳ Up to three servings of foods containing fat and sugar. We all need fat and sugar in our diet, but you should eat these foods only in small quantities. Butter, margarine, oil, mayonnaise, cream, chips, and fried foods are high in fat. Soft drinks, candies, and jelly are high in sugar. Cakes, chocolate, cookies, pastries, and ice cream are high in both. You should generally try to steer clear of these foods while you are on the beach body plan, and focus instead on including small amounts of unsaturated fat such as olive, sunflower, or corn oils in your diet.

Healthy snacking

If you feel the need to snack, here are some bikini-friendly healthy options to choose from. Aim to have no more than two snacks per day and only if you really need them.

✳ Chopped, raw carrot, cucumber, or sweet bell pepper batons dipped in lowfat hummus.

✳ Chunks of avocado, cucumber, or cooked sweet potato.

✳ Two rice cakes topped with lowfat peanut butter.

✳ One pot of lowfat plain yogurt.

✳ One homemade ice pop (made from pure, natural orange juice).

✳ One handful of dried fruit such as prunes, apricots, or papaya.

Breakfast recipes

A good, hearty breakfast is the most important meal of the day. It helps to kick-start your metabolism, and opting for these delicious recipes means you won't feel the need for a mid-morning snack.

Bilberry bircher muesli

SERVES 2
- generous 1 cup jumbo oats
- scant 1 cup apple juice
- 1 red apple, cored
- 1 tbsp lemon juice
- 2 tbsp chopped toasted hazelnuts
- ½ tsp ground cinnamon
- generous ⅓ cup plain yogurt
- 2 tbsp runny honey (optional)
- ½ cup fresh bilberries or blueberries

1 Put the oats and apple juice in a bowl, then cover with plastic wrap and let soak in the refrigerator for an hour. You can do this the night before.

2 Grate or chop the apple and mix it with the lemon juice to prevent discoloration.

3 Add the apple, hazelnuts, and cinnamon to the oat mixture and mix well.

4 Spoon the mixture into serving bowls and top with the yogurt. Drizzle over the honey, if using. Spoon the bilberries over the muesli and serve.

Exotic dried fruit compote

SERVES 4
- generous ¾ cup no-soak dried peaches
- ½ cup no-soak dried apricots
- scant ½ cup no-soak dried pineapple chunks
- ½ cup no-soak dried mango slices
- 1 cup unsweetened clear apple juice
- 4 tbsp lowfat plain yogurt (optional)

1 Put the dried fruit into a small saucepan with the apple juice. Bring slowly to a boil. Reduce the heat to low, then cover and simmer for 10 minutes.

2 Spoon into serving dishes and top each serving with a tablespoon of yogurt, if desired. Serve immediately.

Detox special

SERVES 4
- 1 mango
- 4 kiwi
- 1 ¼ cups pineapple juice
- 4 fresh mint leaves

1 Cut the mango into 2 thick slices as close to the pit as possible. Scoop out the flesh and chop coarsely. Cut off any flesh adhering to the pit. Peel the kiwi with a sharp knife and chop the flesh.

2 Put the mango, kiwi, pineapple juice, and mint leaves in a blender and process until thoroughly combined.

Pour into chilled glasses and serve.

TOP LEFT Bilberry bircher muesli TOP RIGHT Exotic dried fruit compote BOTTOM LEFT Detox special BOTTOM RIGHT Watermelon, orange & ginger cocktail with granola.

Watermelon, orange & ginger cocktail with granola

SERVES 4

FOR THE GRANOLA
1/4 oz/10 g rolled oats
1/8 oz/5 g sesame seeds
pinch of ground ginger
1/8 oz/5 g sunflower seeds
2 tsp freshly squeezed orange juice
1 tsp runny honey

FOR THE FRUIT COCKTAIL
10 1/2 oz/300 g seeded watermelon, cut into chunks
3 1/2 oz/100 g fresh orange segments
6 tbsp freshly squeezed orange juice
1 tsp finely grated orange zest
1 tsp ginger, peeled and finely sliced
1 tsp runny honey
1/2 tsp arrowroot, blended with a little cold water

1 Preheat the oven to 350ºF/180ºC. To make the granola, put all the dry ingredients into a bowl, then add the orange juice and honey and mix thoroughly. Spread out on a nonstick baking sheet and bake for 7–8 minutes.

2 Remove the granola from the oven and break up into pieces, then return to the oven for an additional 7–8 minutes. Remove from the oven and break up again. Let cool on the baking sheet. The mixture will become crunchy when cool.

3 To make the fruit cocktail, put the watermelon and orange segments into a bowl. Put the orange juice and zest, ginger, and honey into a small saucepan over medium heat and bring to a boil. Gradually stir in the arrowroot mixture and cook, stirring constantly, until thickened.

4 Pour the mixture over the fruit and let cool. Cover and chill in the refrigerator. Spoon the fruit into glasses and sprinkle over the granola.

Scrambled eggs with smoked salmon

SERVES 4

8 eggs
1/3 cup light cream
2 tbsp chopped fresh dill, plus extra salt and pepper
3 1/2 oz/100 g smoked salmon, cut into small pieces
2 tbsp butter
4 slices rustic bread, toasted
sprig of dill, for garnish

1 Break the eggs into a large bowl and whisk together with the cream and dill. Season to taste with salt and pepper. Add the smoked salmon and mix to combine.

2 Melt the butter in a large nonstick skillet and pour in the egg and smoked salmon mixture. Using a wooden spatula, gently scrape the egg away from the sides of the skillet as it begins to set and swirl the skillet slightly to let the uncooked egg fill the surface.

3 When the eggs are almost cooked but still creamy, remove from the heat and spoon onto the prepared toast.

Serve immediately, garnished with a sprig of dill.

Carrot & ginger energizer

SERVES 2

generous 1 cup carrot juice
4 tomatoes, skinned, seeded
   and coarsely chopped
1 tbsp lemon juice
$\frac{1}{3}$ cup fresh parsley
1 tbsp grated fresh ginger
6 ice cubes
$\frac{1}{2}$ cup water
chopped fresh flat-leaf parsley,
   for garnish

1 Put the carrot juice, tomatoes, and lemon juice into a food
   processor and process gently until combined.

2 Add the parsley to the food processor along with the ginger and
   ice cubes. Process until well combined, then pour in the water
and process until smooth.

3 Pour the mixture into tall glasses and garnish with chopped
   fresh parsley.

Serve immediately.

Breakfast smoothie

SERVES 2

generous 1 cup orange juice
$\frac{1}{2}$ cup plain yogurt
2 eggs
2 bananas, sliced and frozen, plus extra
   slices of fresh banana, for decorating

1 Pour the orange juice and yogurt into a food processor and
   process gently until combined.

2 Add the eggs and frozen bananas and process until smooth.
   Pour into glasses and decorate with the banana slices.

Lunch recipes

These lunches are healthy but filling. They are also easy to prepare and use inexpensive, everyday ingredients.

Pita pockets with hummus & salad

SERVES 2

2–4 pita breads
1 tsp vinegar
½ tsp Dijon mustard
¼ iceberg lettuce, finely shredded
1 scallion, chopped
½ yellow bell pepper, seeded
  and chopped
1 large tomato, seeded and chopped
2-inch/5-cm piece cucumber, chopped
1 carrot, peeled and grated
FOR THE HUMMUS
14 oz/400 g canned chickpeas, drained
  and liquid reserved
1 garlic clove, chopped
3 tbsp olive oil
2 tbsp tahini
juice of ½ lemon
pepper
pinch of paprika

1 To make the hummus, put the chickpeas, garlic, 2 tablespoons of the oil, the tahini, lemon juice, and a little of the chickpea liquid in a blender or food processor and blend until smooth and creamy. Season to taste with pepper and the paprika. Heat the pita breads and split each one to create a pocket.

2 To make the dressing, whisk the remaining oil with the vinegar and mustard, and pepper to taste, in a pitcher.

3 Mix all the salad ingredients together in a bowl, then add the dressing and toss well to coat. Spread the inside of the pita pockets with the hummus, then fill with the salad and serve. For a lunch box, spread the inside of the unheated pita pockets with hummus, then fill with the undressed salad and wrap well in foil.

Hot & sour noodle & mushroom salad

SERVES 4

250 g/9 oz rice vermicelli noodles
2 tbsp sesame oil
6 scallions
1 ½ cups button mushrooms
½ cucumber
FOR THE DRESSING
4 tbsp sesame oil
2 tbsp Thai fish sauce
juice of 2 limes
1 tsp sugar
1–2 tsp hot chili sauce
2 tbsp chopped fresh cilantro

1 Soak the noodles in a bowl of hot water for 10 minutes, or according to the package directions. Drain and place in a large bowl. Add the sesame oil and toss until the noodles are coated with the oil.

2 Slice the scallions and mushrooms, then cut the cucumber into matchsticks. Add to the noodles in the bowl.

3 To make the dressing, place the sesame oil, fish sauce, lime juice, sugar, and chili sauce in a small bowl and whisk together. Stir in the chopped cilantro.

4 Pour the dressing over the salad and toss until coated. Serve immediately.

TOP LEFT Pita pockets with hummus & salad TOP RIGHT Hot and sour noodle & mushroom salad BOTTOM LEFT Smoked chicken salad with avocado dressing BOTTOM RIGHT Sweet & sour fish salad.

Smoked chicken salad with avocado dressing

SERVES 4

2 large, juicy beefsteak tomatoes, sliced
1 lb 5 oz/600 g smoked chicken, skinned
  and cut into slices
9 oz/250 g fresh watercress, any thick
  stems or yellow leaves removed,
  then rinsed and patted dry
$\frac{1}{2}$ cup fresh bean sprouts, soaked for
  20 minutes in cold water, then drained
  well and patted dry
leaves from several sprigs fresh
  flat-leaf parsley or cilantro

FOR THE DRESSING
1 ripe, soft avocado
2 tbsp lemon juice
1 tbsp tarragon vinegar
$\frac{1}{3}$ cup strained plain yogurt
1 small garlic clove, crushed
1 tbsp chopped fresh tarragon leaves
salt and pepper

1 To make the dressing, put the avocado, lemon juice, and vinegar in a blender or food processor and blend until smooth, scraping down the side with a rubber spatula. Add the yogurt, garlic, and tarragon leaves and process again. Season with salt and pepper to taste, then transfer to a bowl. Cover closely with plastic wrap and chill for 2 hours.

2 To assemble the salad, divide the tomato slices between individual plates. Toss the smoked chicken, watercress, bean sprouts, and parsley or cilantro leaves together. Divide the salad ingredients between the plates.

3 Adjust the seasoning in the dressing, if necessary. Spoon the dressing over each salad and serve.

Sweet & sour fish salad

SERVES 4

8 oz/225 g trout fillets
8 oz/225 g white fish fillets
  (such as haddock or cod)
1 $\frac{1}{4}$ cups water
1 stalk lemon grass
2 lime leaves
1 large red chile
1 bunch scallions, trimmed
  and shredded
generous $\frac{3}{4}$ cup diced fresh
  pineapple flesh
1 small red bell pepper, seeded and diced

1 bunch watercress, washed and trimmed
fresh snipped chives, for garnish
FOR THE DRESSING
1 tbsp sunflower oil
1 tbsp rice wine vinegar
pinch of chili powder
1 tsp clear honey
salt and pepper

1 Rinse the fish, then place in a skillet and pour over the water. Bend the lemon grass in half to bruise it and add to the skillet with the lime leaves. Prick the chile with a fork and add to the skillet. Bring to a boil and simmer for 7–8 minutes. Let cool.

2 Drain the fish fillets thoroughly, then flake the flesh away from the skin and place in a bowl. Gently stir in the scallions, pineapple, and bell pepper.

3 Arrange the washed watercress on 4 serving plates and spoon the cooked fish mixture on top.

4 To make the dressing, mix all the ingredients together, seasoning well. Spoon over the fish and serve garnished with chives.

Parma ham with melon & asparagus

SERVES 4

8 oz/225 g asparagus spears
1 small or ¹/₂ medium-sized Galia or
 cantaloupe melon
2 oz/55 g Parma ham, thinly sliced
5¹/₂-oz/150-g bag mixed salad greens,
 such as herb salad with arugula

generous ¹/₂ cup fresh raspberries
1 tbsp freshly shaved Parmesan cheese
FOR THE DRESSING
1 tbsp balsamic vinegar
2 tbsp raspberry vinegar
2 tbsp orange juice

1 Trim the asparagus, cutting in half if the spears are very long. Cook in lightly salted, boiling water over medium heat for 5 minutes, or until tender. Drain and plunge into cold water, then drain again and reserve.

2 Cut the melon in half and scoop out the seeds. Cut into small wedges and cut away the rind. Separate the Parma ham slices, then cut in half and wrap around the melon wedges.

3 Arrange the salad greens on a large serving platter and place the melon wedges on top, together with the asparagus spears.

4 Scatter over the raspberries and Parmesan shavings. Place the vinegars and juice in a screw-top jar and shake until blended. Pour over the salad and serve.

Leek & potato soup

SERVES 4
- ¹/₂ stick butter
- 1 onion, chopped
- 3 leeks, sliced
- 8 oz/225 g potatoes, peeled and cut into ³/₄-inch/2-cm cubes
- 3³/₄ cups vegetable stock
- salt and pepper
- ²/₃ cup light cream, optional
- 2 tbsp snipped fresh chives, for garnish

1 Melt the butter in a large saucepan over medium heat, then add the prepared vegetables and sauté gently for 2–3 minutes, or until softened but not brown. Pour in the stock and bring to a boil, then reduce the heat and simmer, covered, for 15 minutes.

2 Remove from the heat and blend the soup in the saucepan using a hand-held stick blender if you have one. Otherwise, pour into a food processor, then blend until smooth and return to the rinsed-out saucepan.

3 Heat the soup. Season with salt and pepper and serve in warm bowls, swirled with the cream, if using, and garnished with chives.

Salad niçoise

SERVES 4
- 2 tuna steaks, about ³/₄ inch/2 cm thick
- olive oil
- salt and pepper
- 9 oz/250 g green beans, topped and tailed
- ¹/₂ cup vinaigrette or garlic vinaigrette dressing

- 2 hearts of lettuce, leaves separated
- 3 large hard-cooked eggs, quartered
- 2 large, juicy tomatoes, cut into wedges
- 1³/₄ oz/50 g anchovy fillets in oil, drained
- ¹/₃ cup Niçoise olives, pitted

1 Heat a ridged cast-iron griddle pan over high heat until you can feel the heat rising from the surface. Brush the tuna steaks with oil, then place oiled side down on the hot pan and chargrill for 2 minutes. Lightly brush the top side of the tuna steaks with more oil. Use a pair of tongs to turn the tuna steaks over, then season to taste with salt and pepper. Continue chargrilling for an additional 2 minutes for rare or up to 4 minutes for well done. Let cool.

2 Meanwhile, bring a saucepan of salted water to a boil. Add the beans to the pan and return to a boil, then boil for 3 minutes, or until tender-crisp. Drain the beans and immediately transfer them to a large bowl. Pour over the vinaigrette and stir together, then let the beans cool in the dressing.

3 To serve, line a platter with lettuce leaves. Lift the beans out of the bowl, leaving the excess dressing behind, and pile them in the center of the platter. Break the tuna into large pieces and arrange it over the beans. Arrange the hard-cooked eggs and tomatoes around the side. Place the anchovy fillets over the salad, then scatter with the olives. Drizzle the remaining dressing in the bowl over everything and serve.

Dinner recipes

These delicious dinners will satisfy your hunger and your taste buds without piling on additional weight.

Quick pork & pasta stir-fry

SERVES 2

1 tbsp peanut oil
$\frac{1}{2}$ tsp chili powder, or to taste
2 garlic cloves, crushed
$\frac{1}{2}$ red cabbage, shredded
8 small baby leeks, halved
1 orange bell pepper, sliced thinly
1 carrot, sliced thinly
1 zucchini, sliced thinly
12 oz/350 g pork tenderloin, cubed
cooked fettucine or vermicelli,
    for serving

1 Heat the oil in a large skillet or wok over medium heat and add the chili powder, garlic, and red cabbage. Stir-fry for 2-3 minutes.

2 Stir in the rest of the vegetables and cook for an additional 2 minutes. Add the meat, then increase the heat and stir-fry for about 5 minutes, or until the pork is well cooked and the dish is piping hot.

Serve immediately over fettucine or vermicelli.

TOP LEFT Quick pork and pasta stir fry TOP RIGHT Teriyaki salmon fillets with Chinese noodles BOTTOM LEFT Stuffed red bell peppers with basil BOTTOM RIGHT Roasted butternut-squash risotto.

Teriyaki salmon fillets with Chinese noodles

SERVES 4

4 salmon fillets, about 7 oz/200 g each
$\frac{1}{2}$ cup teriyaki marinade
1 shallot, sliced
$\frac{3}{4}$-inch/2-cm piece fresh ginger,
    finely chopped
2 carrots, sliced
4 oz/115 g closed-cup mushrooms, sliced
5 cups vegetable stock
9 oz/250 g dried medium egg noodles
1 cup frozen peas
6 oz/175 g Chinese cabbage, shredded
4 scallions, sliced

1 Wipe off any scales from the salmon skin. Arrange the salmon fillets, skin-side up, in a single layer. Mix the teriyaki marinade with the shallot and ginger in a small bowl and pour over the salmon. Cover and let marinate in the refrigerator for at least 1 hour, turning the salmon over halfway through the marinating time.

2 Put the carrots, mushrooms, and stock into a large saucepan. Arrange the salmon, skin-side down, on a shallow baking sheet. Pour the fish marinade into the saucepan of vegetables and stock and bring to a boil. Reduce the heat, then cover and simmer for 10 minutes.

3 Meanwhile, preheat the broiler to medium. Cook the salmon under the preheated broiler for 10-15 minutes, depending on the thickness of the fillets, until the flesh turns pink and flakes easily. Remove from the broiler and keep warm.

4 Add the noodles and peas to the stock and return to a boil. Reduce the heat, then cover and simmer for 5 minutes, or until the noodles are tender. Stir in the Chinese cabbage and scallions and heat through for 1 minute.

5 Carefully drain off $1\frac{1}{4}$ cups of the stock into a small heatproof pitcher and reserve. Drain and discard the remaining stock. Divide the noodles and vegetables between 4 warmed serving bowls and top each with a salmon fillet. Pour the reserved stock over each bowl and serve immediately.

Stuffed red bell peppers with basil

SERVES 4

scant ³/₄ cup long-grain white or
  brown rice
4 large red bell peppers
2 tbsp olive oil
1 garlic clove, chopped
4 shallots, chopped
1 celery stick, chopped
3 tbsp chopped toasted walnuts

2 tomatoes, peeled and chopped
1 tbsp lemon juice
scant ¹/₃ cup raisins
4 tbsp freshly grated Cheddar cheese
2 tbsp chopped fresh basil
salt and pepper
fresh basil sprigs, for garnish
lemon wedges, for serving

1 Preheat the oven to 350ºF/180ºC. Cook the rice in a saucepan of lightly salted boiling water for 20 minutes if using white rice, or 35 minutes if using brown. Drain, then rinse under cold running water and drain again.

2 Cut the tops off the bell peppers and reserve. Remove the seeds and white cores, then blanch the bell peppers and tops in boiling water for 2 minutes. Remove from the heat and drain well. Heat half the oil in a large skillet. Add the garlic and shallots and cook, stirring, for 3 minutes.

Add the celery, walnuts, tomatoes, lemon juice, and raisins and cook for an additional 5 minutes. Remove from the heat and stir in the cheese, chopped basil, and seasoning.

3 Stuff the bell peppers with the rice mixture and arrange them in a baking dish. Place the reserved tops on the bell peppers and drizzle over the remaining oil, then loosely cover with foil and bake in the preheated oven for 45 minutes. Remove the stuffed peppers from the oven.

Garnish with basil sprigs and serve with lemon wedges.

Roasted butternut-squash risotto

SERVES 4

1 lb 5 oz/600 g butternut squash
  or pumpkin, peeled and cut into
  bite-sized pieces
4 tbsp olive oil
1 tsp clear honey
generous ¹/₄ cup fresh basil
generous ¹/₄ cup fresh oregano

1 tbsp margarine
2 onions, finely chopped
2¹/₄ cups Arborio or other risotto rice
³/₄ cup dry white wine
5 cups hot vegetable stock
salt and pepper

1 Preheat the oven to 400ºF/200ºC. Put the squash into a roasting pan. Mix 1 tablespoon of the oil with the honey and spoon over the squash. Turn the squash to coat it in the mixture. Roast in the preheated oven for 30-35 minutes, or until tender.

2 Meanwhile, put the basil and oregano into a food processor with 2 tablespoons of the remaining oil and process until finely chopped and blended. Set aside.

3 Heat the margarine and remaining oil in a large, heavy-bottom saucepan over medium heat. Add the onions and cook, stirring occasionally, for 8 minutes, or until softened and golden. Add the rice and cook for 2 minutes. Stir to coat the grains in the oil mixture.

4 Pour in the wine and bring to a boil. Reduce the heat slightly and cook until the wine is almost absorbed. Add the stock, a little at a time, and cook over medium-low heat, stirring constantly, for 20 minutes.

5 Gently stir in the herb oil and squash until thoroughly mixed into the rice and cook for an additional 5 minutes, or until the rice is creamy and cooked but retaining a little bite in the center of the grain. Season well with salt and pepper before serving.

Chargrilled swordfish

SERVES 4

4 swordfish steaks,
 about 5½ oz/150 g each
salt and pepper
fresh cilantro and lime wedges,
 for garnish
freshly cooked baked potatoes,
 corn-on-the-cob, and fresh arugula
 leaves, for serving

FOR THE MARINADE

3 tbsp rice wine or sherry
3 tbsp chili oil
2 garlic cloves,
 finely chopped
juice of 1 lime
1 tbsp chopped fresh
 cilantro

1 To make the marinade, put the rice wine, oil, garlic, lime juice, and cilantro into a bowl and mix together well.

2 Rinse the fish steaks under cold running water, then pat dry with paper towels. Arrange the fish in a shallow, non-metallic (glass or ceramic) dish, which will not react with acid. Season with salt and pepper, then pour over the marinade and turn the fish in the mixture until well coated. Cover with plastic wrap and refrigerate for 1½ hours.

3 Meanwhile, place a ridged cast-iron frying pan over high heat until you can feel the heat rising from the surface. When the fish is thoroughly marinated, lift out of the marinade, then place on the hot pan and chargrill for 4 minutes. Turn the fish over, then brush with more marinade and chargrill on the other side for another 4 minutes, or until cooked through.

4 Remove from the heat and garnish with chopped fresh cilantro and slices of lime. Serve with hot baked potatoes, corn-on-the-cob, and fresh arugula leaves.

Vegetable chili

SERVES 4

1 eggplant, cut into 1-inch/2.5-cm slices
1 tbsp olive oil, plus extra for brushing
1 large red or yellow onion,
  finely chopped
2 red or yellow bell peppers,
  seeded and finely chopped
3–4 garlic cloves, finely chopped
  or crushed
1 lb 12 oz/800 g canned
  chopped tomatoes
1 tbsp mild chili powder

$^{1}/_{2}$ tsp ground cumin
$^{1}/_{2}$ tsp dried oregano
2 small zucchini, quartered lengthwise
  and sliced
salt and pepper
14 oz/400 g canned kidney beans,
  drained and rinsed
scant 2 cups water
1 tbsp tomato paste
6 scallions, finely chopped
1 cup grated Cheddar cheese

1 Brush the eggplant slices on one side with oil. Heat half the oil in a large, heavy-bottom skillet over medium heat. Add the eggplant slices, oiled-side down, and cook for 5–6 minutes, or until browned on one side. Turn the slices over and cook on the other side until browned, then transfer to a plate. Cut into bite-size pieces.

2 Heat the remaining oil in a large skillet over medium heat. Add the onion and bell peppers and cook, stirring frequently, for 3–4 minutes, or until the onion is just softened. Add the garlic and cook, stirring frequently, for an additional 2–3 minutes, or until the onion is beginning to color.

3 Add the tomatoes, chili powder, cumin, and oregano and season to taste with salt and pepper. Bring just to a boil, then reduce the heat and simmer gently, covered, for 15 minutes.

4 Add the zucchini, eggplant pieces, beans, water, and tomato paste to the skillet and return to a boil. Reduce the heat, then cover and simmer for an additional 45 minutes, or until the vegetables are tender. Taste and adjust the seasoning, if necessary.

Ladle into warmed bowls and top with the scallions and cheese.

Roasted chicken with sun-blush tomato pesto

SERVES 4

4 skinless, boneless chicken breasts,
  about 1 lb 12 oz/800 g in total
1 tbsp olive oil
green salad and crusty bread,
  for serving
FOR THE RED PESTO
$^{3}/_{4}$ cup sun-blush tomatoes in oil
  (drained), chopped
2 garlic cloves, crushed
6 tbsp pine nuts, lightly toasted
$^{2}/_{3}$ cup extra-virgin olive oil

1 Preheat the oven to 400°F/200°C. To make the red pesto, put the sun-blush tomatoes, garlic, 4 tablespoons of the pine nuts, and the oil into a food processor and blend to a coarse paste.

2 Arrange the chicken in a large, ovenproof dish or roasting pan. Brush each breast with the oil, then place a tablespoon of red pesto over each breast. Using the back of a spoon, spread the pesto

so that it covers the top of each breast. (This pesto recipe makes more than just the four tablespoons used here. Store the extra pesto in an airtight container in the refrigerator for up to 1 week.)

3 Roast the chicken in the preheated oven for 30 minutes, or until tender and the juices run clear when a skewer is inserted into the thickest part of the meat.

4 Sprinkle with the remaining pine nuts and serve with a green side salad and crusty bread.

Getting fit

You've given your body the right fuel to get it working at its optimum capacity—now it's time to tone up those muscles so that you're happy to reveal it on the beach. These exercises are designed to tone up the parts of your body that show in a bikini: your stomach, chest, and thighs. You should spend time warming up before you start (and cooling down when you finish).

Getting fit

You don't have to be stick thin to look sexy in a bikini. Swimwear looks great on women with curves, and you should be proud of yours. But if you are aiming to lose a few pounds or to tone up before you hit the beach, the exercises in this section will help you to achieve your goal.

Confidence is key

Even if you're usually quite active and are confident about the way you look, stripping down to your swimwear can come as a bit of a shock to the system. Bits of your body that usually never see the light of day under "normal" circumstances–think thighs, stomach, and chest–are suddenly exposed to the whole world. The important thing to remember is that you are your own worst critic and any perceived flaws or wobbly bits you have are much less likely to even register with others–they are far more concerned about how they look!

The first rule is to stop worrying. If you're more accepting of your body shape, you can learn how to accentuate your good points. For example, if you are of average height (around 5ft 4in), don't waste time lusting after a long and leggy look. Instead, focus on enhancing your curvy waist–it is a far more realistic goal.

The exercises in this section have been carefully chosen to help you target trouble zones such as thighs, hips, stomach, and arms, which are typically on show on the beach. If you focus on toning up these areas and combine the exercises with general cardiovascular work, it will have more of an impact on how you look in your bikini. It's like taking a short cut to a better body.

Jump to it

All the exercises in this book are easy to follow and are designed to give maximum results. You should spend some time reading the directions and testing out each one so you know exactly what's required and will be ready to go as soon as you start the plan. All the exercises can be done at home–essential if you haven't got a lot of time to fit activity into your daily schedule.

You'll need to clear a space where you can do your exercise–choose somewhere that gives you enough room to fully extend your arms and legs, so you won't risk injuring yourself by colliding with the furniture. You don't need any specialized equipment in order to carry out the exercises. A pair of supportive tennis shoes and some stretchy jogging pants and a top will do the job nicely. If a certain exercise requires a piece of equipment, such as a step or some hand weights, you'll be advised in the directions, but we don't ask for anything that couldn't be found in the average home–cans of soup, for example, make excellent hand weights!

It's important to feel comfortable while carrying out the exercises. As with any new exercise regime, you should speak to your physician before you start to rule out any reasons why it wouldn't be suitable for you. If, for any reason, you feel discomfort, light-headed, or faint while carrying out any of the exercises, you should stop and seek the advice of your physician as soon as possible.

As with all forms of exercise, it's really important that you spend time warming up before you start (and cooling down when you finish). Try forward bends, side bends, knee bends, or leg swings to warm up and full body stretches to cool down.

Your body, only better

The great thing about exercising is that it can have a real impact on your body shape and boost the results you get from healthy eating. Some of the movements target specific muscle groups and require you to repeat them over and over again. This works the muscles sufficiently for you to "feel the burn." It's generally a good thing, but if you are in any pain at all, stop doing what you're doing and seek the advice of a medic as soon as you can.

As you learn how to do the different exercises by heart, you'll be able to do them anywhere and at any time. This means you can keep up your regime wherever you happen to be, making the plan really easy to stick to. Most exercises in this book take around six minutes to complete, but you should aim for at least 20 minutes of exercise each day. As well as completing your daily beach-body toning exercise, make sure you are active in other ways. Try power walking for 20 minutes, jogging in the open air, joining a dance class or tennis club, or simply taking the stairs instead of the lift at work. The more you do, the bigger the difference it will make to your shape. Make sure you choose an activity you enjoy because you are then more likely to continue doing it.

Being active—the benefits

Exercise is not only good for toning up your muscles. Here is a run down of all the fantastic benefits you'll get from being more active...

❋ It will boost your metabolism. These exercises focus on toning up certain areas of your body, such as the stomach and thighs. The ones that require some form of resistance work will help you shed fat and replace it with lean muscle, causing you to lose weight more quickly. This is because, in its resting state, muscle burns more calories than fat. So even while you sleep, your body will be working to get you ready for your beach holiday.

❋ You'll look younger. As well as the fantastic side effect of dropping a few pounds, exercise could help to turn back the clock. Exercise gets your heart rate going which, in turn, pumps blood around the body, giving your skin a healthy pink glow. The skin absorbs vital nutrients in the blood, which help to feed and repair skin cells, leaving you with a more youthful-looking complexion.

❋ It will regulate your appetite. Many people think that exercising regularly will increase their appetite, but often the opposite is true. Exercise, when it's done correctly, actually suppresses the appetite, meaning you could forgo that afternoon snack. If you are exercising well, you will be drinking more water too, which can help keep hunger pangs at bay (many are actually caused by dehydration rather than hunger in the first place). You might also find that being good to your body, by exercising, makes you crave healthier foods as your body tries desperately to let you know what nutrients it needs to replace the lost energy. And if your body's asking for a plate of spinach, who are you to argue?

❋ It will boost your mood. Exercising might seem like a drag at times, but being active encourages the brain to release the "happy hormone," seratonin. This is why many people find exercising to be quite addictive, due to the "high" you get afterward.

Seated knee lift

This easy exercise can be performed when you're sitting at your desk or even when traveling. It's great for a quick stomach-toning session and for postural realignment. You'll need a straight-backed, sturdy chair–not one on casters.

It will work your rectus abdominis–the muscle that runs down the front of your stomach. Make sure your movements are controlled and flowing.

1 Sit on the edge of a chair with your knees bent and pressed together and your feet flat on the floor. Hold on to the sides of the chair, then tighten your stomach muscles.

2 Lean back slightly and lift your feet a few inches off the ground, keeping your knees bent and pressed together. Slowly pull your knees in toward your chest and curl your upper body forward. Then lower your feet to the floor.

3 Rest for a count of three before you do any repetitions.

1

2

Top tip

✳ Don't lean too far forward, or you'll fall off the chair!

1

2

Spine rotation

This exercise gently mobilizes your spine, preparing it for harder exercises to come.

1 Sit forward on a chair with your back straight and your hands resting on your thighs. Your knees should be over your ankles. Tighten your abdominal muscles.

2 Keeping your hips and knees forward, slowly rotate your upper body to the left until you can put both hands on the back of the chair. Hold for a count of ten, then return to the center. Repeat the exercise, twisting to the right.

Top tip

✳ Twist only as far as is comfortable.

Belly tightener

Exercising in this position means you are working against gravity, making your muscles work even harder. Remember to keep your elbows soft, not locked.

This is also known as abdominal hollowing and helps to shorten the abdominal muscles, which is good for your posture and creates the appearance of a flatter stomach.

1 Kneel down on all fours (the "box" position) with your hands shoulder-width apart, your elbows slightly bent, and your knees under your hips. Keep your head in line with the rest of your body and look down at the floor, making sure that your chin isn't tucked into your chest.

2 Relax your abdominal muscles, then slowly draw in your navel toward your spine.

3 Hold the muscles in for a count of ten, then slowly relax. Breathe slowly and steadily throughout this exercise.

Top tip

✳ Pull up the abdomen by using your deep abdominal muscles, not by arching your spine.

1

2

Easy plank (tension hold)

Holding your body in a three-quarters plank shape strengthens the deep transverse muscles that cross the stomach area. Keeping your knees on the floor makes this exercise much easier than the traditional plank, which you can progress to when you feel ready.

1 Adopt a traditional press-up position, but keep your knees on the floor and your feet in the air. Your fingers should point forward, your elbows should stay straight, but not locked, your head should be in line with your body, and your feet together. Keep your shoulder blades drawn into your back and make sure you don't dip in the middle or raise your buttocks in the air.

2 Hold this position for a count of ten, breathing regularly throughout.

HOW TO BREATHE PROPERLY

Breathing is something we all take for granted, but most of us only ever use the top third of our lungs. Learn to breathe properly, and it's probably the best thing you can do for your overall health, because oxygen nourishes and replenishes all your body's cells. Abdominal breathing is a technique that enables you to breathe more deeply. It uses the diaphragm, the sheet of muscle forming the top of the abdomen, to help the lungs inflate and deflate effortlessly. Breathe in slowly through your nose, and notice how the top of the abdomen rises as you do so. Hold the breath for a few seconds, then breathe out slowly through your mouth.

Top tip

✳ Avoid this exercise if you have shoulder problems. If you feel any strain in your back muscles, move your knees farther apart.

2

Lower abdominal raise

This exercise will tighten the abdominal muscles without putting any strain on your back. It's a simple way to tone and strengthen your abdominal muscles. If it seems easy, you're not doing it properly!

1 Lie on your back with your knees bent, feet flat on the floor and hip-width apart. Make sure your spine is in neutral. Keep your arms by your sides with the palms facing upward.

2 Lift your legs into the air at an angle of 90° to your body.

3 Tighten your abdominal muscles and slowly lower one foot to the floor, then bring it back up again. Repeat this exercise using the other leg.

3

2

Moving curl

This exercise gives your rectus abdominis—the muscle that runs down the front of your stomach—an intensive workout, by repeating the hardest part of the abdominal curl. As you lift your head and shoulders, this muscle contracts at both ends. Avoid this exercise if you have neck problems.

1 Lie on your back with your feet flat on the floor, knees bent and your palms on your thighs. Keep your spine in neutral. Tighten your abdominal muscles.

2 Start curling up by lifting your head and shoulder blades off the floor while reaching forward with your arms.

3 Curl up about 30° off the floor. Then extend your arms and lift and lower yourself just a few inches up and down from this position.

4 Repeat several times, then lower yourself back down to the floor and relax.

Tips for great curls

* Always keep your knees slightly bent (flexed).

* Breathe out as you curl up and breathe in on the return.

* Never hold your breath when exercising—your blood pressure will rise and this can be dangerous.

* Perform all exercises in a slow, controlled manner.

* Don't put your hands behind your neck, because you are likely to tug on the neck vertebrae.

Basic oblique curl

Twisting curls work your rectus abdominis muscles and the obliques, the muscles that give definition to the waist. This exercise will tighten your stomach muscles and trim your waist.

1 Lie on your back with your knees bent, feet flat on the floor and hip-width apart. Put your hands by your temples at the sides of your head. Lift your left leg and rest the ankle of that leg across your right thigh—this will turn your supported left leg out slightly. Keep your spine in neutral and tighten your abdominal muscles.

2 Curl up, rotating your trunk to the left and breathing out as you do so. Your right elbow should be moving toward your left knee. Keep your left side in contact with the floor to help support your back.

3 Curl back down again, breathing in as you do so. Repeat this exercise to the other side, using the other leg.

Basic reverse curl

Reverse curls give a good workout to the transversus abdominis, the deepest abdominal muscle that wraps around your waist like a corset, and the rectus abdominis, the stomach muscle that's responsible for the six-pack look. Remember not to arch your back as you do this exercise.

1 Lie on your back with your spine in neutral. You can keep your arms by your sides, palms facing downward, or by the sides of your head. Tuck your knees in toward your stomach and cross your ankles.

2 Tighten your abdominal muscles by gently pulling your navel in towards your spine.

3 Roll your knees toward your chest, then lower them down again.

HOW MUSCLES WORK

Here's the science: muscles are made up of millions of tiny protein filaments that relax and contract to produce movement. Most muscles are attached to bones by tendons and are consciously controlled by your brain. Electrical signals from the brain travel via nerves to the muscles, causing the cells within the muscle to contract. Movement happens when muscles pull on tendons, which move the bones at the joints. Muscles work in pairs, enabling bones to move in two directions, and most movements require the use of several muscle groups.

Side reach

The small controlled movements in this exercise will work your stomach muscles really hard.

1 Lie on your back with your spine in neutral, your knees bent, feet flat on the floor, hip-width apart, and palms down and by your sides. Tighten your abdominal muscles.

2 Lift your head and shoulders off the floor to an angle of 30˚. Hold this position and reach out with your right hand toward your right calf.

3 Gently move back and forth ten times, then curl back down again. Remember to breathe regularly throughout the exercise.

4 Repeat this exercise, reaching out with the left hand toward the left calf. Gradually build up the number of reaches you can do.

Double-leg push-out

This exercise works the transverse (deep) abdominal muscles as you extend your legs.

1 Sit on the floor with your knees bent and your feet parallel, toes just touching the floor but heels lifted off it.

2 Lean back slightly and support yourself by placing your hands behind you, palms downward on the floor.

3 Tighten your abdominal muscles, holding the rest of your body still.

4 Extend both legs in front of you but do not straighten your legs completely. Bring them back to the starting position.

2

4

Pillow roll

This exercise tones and strengthens your obliques and is a safe way to mobilize your spine. Your shoulders and arms should stay on the floor throughout, but you may find that the opposite arm and shoulder come up slightly when you're still learning the exercise.

1 Lie on your back on the floor with your arms out to the sides at shoulder height, palms flat on the floor. Keep your knees bent. Your feet should be touching and off the floor. To make this exercise easier, you can keep your feet on the floor throughout if you need to.

2 Put a cushion or pillow between your knees –this will make you keep your knees together, which is important for this exercise. Tighten your abdominal muscles.

3 Slowly bend your legs toward the floor on your right side, rolling your head to the left as you do so. Feel each part of your body peel up as you move– your buttocks, then hips, then waist and ribs. Keep going until your right knee and foot are touching the floor with your left leg lying on top.

4 Move your knees and head back to the central position. Repeat on the other side.

2

3

Single-leg squat

Squats are extremely effective. They work the hip extensors, hamstrings (at the back of the thigh muscles), and quadriceps (the front of the thigh muscles) all at once. Tight quads and hamstrings cause poor posture and lower-back pain, so it's very important to keep them in good working order. This squat really challenges your balance as well as working your hips and thigh muscles.

1 Standing with your feet together and your arms by your sides, shift your weight onto your right foot. Rest the toes of your left foot next to your right foot for balance.

2 Keeping your back straight, bend at the hips and knees and slowly sit back onto your right leg, raising your arms in front of you as you lower. Sit back only as far as is comfortable. Stop and hold for a count of two.

3 Now press into your right foot through the heels and come back up.

4 Repeat the exercise with the weight on your left foot.

2

Top tip

* Keep your abdominal muscles tight throughout the exercise.

Basic lunge

Lunges are great for firming your hips and thighs, because they work the hip extensors, quadriceps, and hamstrings. They're also good exercises to help you improve your balance. When you have become adept at performing lunges, you can hold weights in each hand to increase the workout and you can even do walking lunges, provided that your workout space is big enough, or you are able to turn mid-stride!

This is a fabulous hip and thigh toner that is extremely versatile, because you can hold it for increasing amounts of time. Keep your back straight at all times and keep your movements smooth and fluid.

1 Stand up straight with good posture and your hands on your hips. Tighten your abdominal muscles by gently drawing your navel toward your spine, and tense your buttock muscles.

2 Take a big step forward. Your back leg should be long and slightly bent at the knee, with the heel off the floor; the front leg should have the knee over the ankle.

3 Dip your lower body down as far as is comfortable. Hold for a count of two.

4 Push your body all the way back up to the standing position using your front leg. Do all your repetitions on one leg, then switch legs and repeat on the other side.

2

Top tip

✳ Don't lunge too deeply—if you let your knee go beyond the line of the end of your toes, you will put too much stress on your knee joint.

Simple seated thigh squeeze

Even if you're office-bound for a large part of the day or spend a lot of time traveling, you can still sneak in a few exercises to keep your hips and thigh muscles toned. You'll need a straight-backed, sturdy chair for this exercise, which tones and strengthens your inner thighs. Make this exercise harder by increasing the time of the squeeze and by using something with more resistance than a cushion, such as a semi-inflated ball.

1 Sit up straight on a chair with your knees bent and feet together.

2 Place a cushion between your thighs. Squeeze the cushion as hard as possible for a count of five, then release.

2

Double knee bends

This traditional ballet exercise gives a great workout to the legs and buttocks. It strengthens your thighs, calves, and buttocks, and will help you achieve the sculpted legs of a dancer. Keep your movements controlled and flowing.

1 Stand with your legs a little wider than shoulder-width apart and your feet slightly turned out. Rest your hands on the back of a chair to help you keep your balance. Tighten your abdominal muscles to protect your lower back.

2 Slowly press your knees out and lower yourself down. You should feel this in your buttocks and back of your thighs.

3 Return to standing, then tense your buttocks, squeeze your inner thigh muscles, and rise up onto your toes. Return to the start position.

3

2

One-legged buttock clencher

This is a harder exercise that will really work your gluteal muscles.

1 Lie on your back with your knees bent and your feet flat on the floor, slightly apart. Keep your arms by your sides, palms facing downward. Place your left foot on to your right knee. Tighten your abdominal muscles to support your back.

2 Press your lower back down into the floor and gently tilt your pelvis forward so that the pubic bone rises. Lift your hips off the floor and squeeze your buttock muscles, then release.

3 Do all your repetitions on one leg, then repeat on the other leg.

1

2

Bridge squeeze

As well as tightening up your gluteal muscles, this bridging exercise will help to stabilize your pelvis and your trunk muscles, and work your hamstrings. Take care not to overarch your back or let it sag, and remember to keep your breathing steady and controlled throughout.

1 Lie on your back with your knees bent and feet slightly apart.

2 Tighten your abdominal muscles by gently drawing in your navel toward your spine (this will protect your back muscles).

3 Curl your buttocks off the floor, lifting your pelvis until your knees, hips, and chest are in line.

4 Hold this for a count of ten, squeezing your buttock muscles to support the bridge position. Release and repeat.

3

Leg lift

Exercising on all fours makes your muscles work harder because they're working against gravity. Keep all movements smooth and controlled for the best results, and don't let your back sag or arch. This is a lateral thigh raise that works the outer thigh muscles (hip abductors).

1 To start, kneel in the "box" position (on all fours) and keep your back straight. Tighten your abdominal muscles to support your back.

2 Lift your right leg out to the side—you will feel the muscles at the side of the thigh and hip working to lift your leg. Hold for a count of two.

3 Slowly lower your leg to the start position. Do all your repetitions on one leg, then repeat using the other leg.

1

2

Kneeling kick-back

This exercise works your quadriceps—the muscles on the front of your thigh.

1 Get down on all fours and pull in your stomach muscles to protect your back.

2 Raise your right leg off the floor, and with your knee bent, bring it into your body, then stretch it out backward so that it is in line with your body with the foot flexed.

3 Pull the leg back in and take it back out again. Do all your repetitions on one leg, then repeat using the other leg.

Outer thigh lift

This side-lying exercise works the abductor muscles at the side of the thighs. Remember to keep your back straight, your hips facing forward, and to breathe regularly throughout. Make sure you perform each move slowly and in a controlled way to really work the muscles. You don't have to tense your buttocks as you do this, but it's good to work your gluteals whenever you can.

1 Lie on your right side with your body in a straight line and your thighs and feet together. Prop yourself up with your right arm and rest your left hand on the floor in front of you. Tighten your stomach muscles by drawing your navel in toward your spine—this will help to protect your back.

2 Bend both knees. Lift up your top leg, then lower it, squeezing your buttocks together as you raise and lower your leg.

3 Do all your repetitions on one side, then repeat on the other side of your body.

> ### *Top tip*
> ✳ Keep the knee of the extended leg soft (slightly bent).

2

Inner thigh lift

This exercise will work your inner thigh muscles (abductors). Remember to keep your spine in neutral and your stomach muscles tightened throughout.

1 Lie on one side with your hips facing forward and your body in a straight line. Prop yourself up on your elbow with your head resting on your hand and place the other hand on the floor in front of you for support.

2 Tighten your stomach muscles by gently drawing in your navel toward your spine to protect your back.

3 Bend your top leg so that the knee touches the floor in front of you.

4 Raise the bottom extended leg, keeping the knee soft (slightly bent), then lower.

5 Do all your repetitions on one side, then repeat on the other side.

Be a beach beauty

Looking good in a bikini takes more than just losing some weight, toning up your muscles, and pulling in your stomach. Gorgeous, glowing skin and luscious locks will add the finishing touches to your fabulous new look. This chapter is packed full of tips and strategies to help you look your best from top to toe. Good luck—and enjoy!

Get gorgeous and glowing

To be a true beach babe, you need to pay close attention to your skin and hair as well as your figure. This section is packed with tips and tricks to help you look great in the sun—including some that you can do during the lead-up to your holiday, and others for maintaining your looks when you're there.

The final touches

Few women are blessed with naturally glossy hair and flawless skin—this sort of polish takes time and effort to achieve. Mastering some of the expert tricks of the trade will really make a difference to how you look. Our "beach babe" tips take minutes to master, so it won't be hard to squeeze one into your daily schedule, as we recommend in the four-week planner. If you have a specific hair or skin problem, you may want to focus more on the tips that aim to solve it. But it is definitely worth trying out all the tips in this section to prime and prepare you for your holiday.

Natural is best

Many of the beauty recipes in this chapter use ingredients you can find in your store cupboards. Not only are these natural ingredients much more effective than some purpose-made products but they will open your eyes to how easy and cheap it is to take care of your looks.

You should enjoy the time spent pampering yourself. It's a wonderful free way to indulge, without piling on additional weight. And when you see the results—for example, the gorgeous glowing skin you'll have after exfoliating—the effort will definitely seem worthwhile.

Aromatherapy

Consult your physician if you are pregnant, breastfeeding, have skin allergies, high blood pressure, are epileptic, have liver damage, cancer, or any other medical problem before you use any of the aromatherapy recipes in this chapter.

While you're away

The beach is brimming with skin and hair enemies that can spoil your look. Here's what you should be watching out for.

✳ Humidity: If you're prone to frizzy hair, humidity is your worst enemy. When the air is moist, frizz-prone hairs (which are typically more porous) soak up moisture and begin to curl as a result. To beat humidity, try using one of the hair serums that are available in most drugstores—they help seal the hair shaft so it can't absorb as much moisture. If your locks are seriously out of control, practise different "up-do's" that will give you a shabby chic look—a low bun, ponytail, or loose braid will all look beach-gorgeous.

✳ Chlorine: This chemical is commonly used in pools to help clean the water, but it can be damaging to the hair. If you have colored hair, you should consider wearing a swimming cap, as chlorine has a drying effect, which can lead to color fading. Blonds especially should beware; the chemical has a tendency to turn fair tones an unsightly shade of green. Always shampoo and rinse your hair after swimming and apply a nourishing leave-in conditioner or protective serum to keep moisture locked in and your hair color vibrant.

✳ UV rays: As well as being responsible for skin damage, UV rays can also wreak havoc with your hair. Make sure you wear a sun cream with an SPF of at least 15 and a UVA/UVB filter. To save your hair from drying out, apply a heat-protective hair oil and wear a wide-brimmed sun hat or a silk hair scarf while you're out and about in the sun.

✳ Salt water: Salty seawater also has a drying effect on the skin and hair, but it becomes a problem only if you forget to rinse it off, and it becomes dry and crusty in the heat. Each time you go for a cooling dip, remember to finish off with an invigorating shower to remove all traces of salt. A post-swim shower also helps the material that your bikini's made of to keep its color for longer.

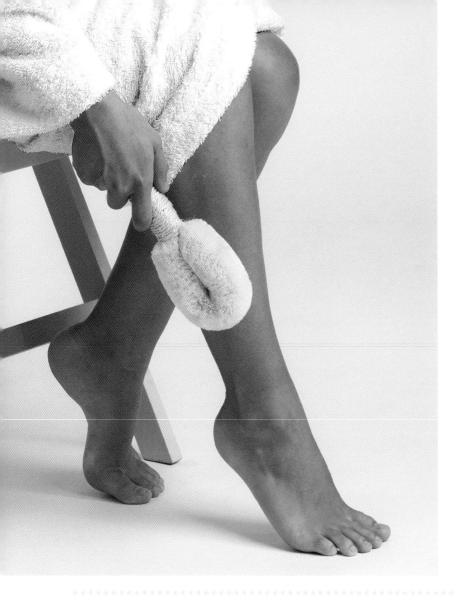

Be beautifully buff

Dry skin brushing is a great way to give your circulation a boost and improve the look of your skin. It is especially effective at getting rid of bumpy skin on the backs of your arms and at tackling the appearance of cellulite. The best time to do it is before you have a shower. You'll need a high-quality dry skin brush with soft bristles, which you can find in any good drugstore or beauty store. Start at the feet and, using a light but firm touch, start to sweep the brush in small circular motions over the skin. Move over the toes and up the legs, toward the hips. Next, start at the fingertips and continue up toward the heart. Go gently over delicate areas such as the neck, so as not to risk damaging the skin. When you've finished, get in the shower and lather yourself with a moisturizing shower gel. Your complexion should be left with a pink, healthy glow.

Make a toning body scrub

The key to soft, smooth skin is regular exfoliation. It helps to get rid of dead skin cells, so your complexion will appear more radiant. It's also the perfect way to prepare for self-tanning, as it will ensure a more even color. Your skin will also be primed to absorb all the nourishing ingredients in your moisturizer.

1 Place 3 tablespoons fine sea salt in a small bowl; add 6 drops grapefruit essential oil and stir in. Get in the shower, but do not turn the water on yet.

2 Take a handful of the mixture and rub it briskly all over your body, paying special attention to your thighs and stomach.

3 Rinse off the skin well.

Grapefruit is cleansing and detoxifying, and the sea salt is an excellent exfoliator, removing loose, dead cells and leaving the skin glowing and ready for moisturizing.

Scrub your skin soft

This unperfumed shower gel gives a lathering base; peppermint and rosemary are cleansing and refreshing herbs; sea salt provides the exfoliation and the olive oil adds a skin-nourishing touch to the body scrub. For 2 applications, you need 4 tablespoons unperfumed shower gel.

1 Pour this into a small dish and add 2 tablespoons very finely chopped peppermint and rosemary leaves, 1 tablespoon fine sea salt, and 1 tablespoon extra-virgin olive oil.

2 Stir these ingredients together well. Rub over the body, especially over problem areas, so you are energized and invigorated.

This works well if you get in the shower and let warm water run over the skin before working up the body scrub to a lather. Reduce the water temperature, letting the jets pummel your body. Change back to warm and apply more of the body scrub and work into the skin. Rinse off and towel yourself dry.

DIY hydrotherapy

Hydrotherapy is often offered in spas as an invigorating treatment that can help to improve the appearance of the skin by toning, tightening, and stimulating the lymphatic system. You can try the hot and cold hydrotherapy method in the comfort of your own bathroom.

First, get in the shower and let the water run comfortably warm; use a little shower cream to lather up on the skin. Then change the temperature of the water to run much cooler, letting the jets pummel your body, particularly your chest, stomach, buttocks, and thighs. This is particularly effective if you have a power shower. Change the temperature back to warm again, and this time massage in some of the grapefruit & sea salt body scrub, using a cellulite massager to really work it into the skin. Finally, rinse off all the scrub, and towel yourself dry. You should feel invigorated and refreshed, with soft, glowing skin.

De-fuzz

Having silky smooth skin is an essential part of any beach beauty's armory. Shaving is by far the quickest and cheapest way to de-fuzz your body. It's best to use a gel or foam, so the razor glides over your skin, making nips and cuts less likely. You should shave in the opposite direction from that in which your hair grows to get as close a shave as possible. You'll be silky smooth for a few days before you'll have to tackle re-growth, so remember to pack some disposable razors in your suitcase.

Sugaring is similar to waxing although it's thought to be less painful because the sugar mixture sticks only to the hair, as opposed to the skin. It's made of natural ingredients and, while you can buy it pre-made in the stores, you can also make it yourself at home. Simply cook two cups of white, processed sugar with a cup of water and a cup of lemon juice on the stove until the mixture forms a stiff paste. Dust the area of skin you want to de-fuzz with talcum powder, then apply the mixture with a spatula. Apply a piece of cloth or absorbent paper onto the mixture, then quickly pull it away in the opposite direction of hair growth, taking the hairs with it. The results should last for up to one week.

Waxing is the most effective, but perhaps the most painful way to remove body hair. You can buy ready-prepared waxing strips in most drugstores, or pots of liquid wax, which you warm to melt before you use it. Waxing pulls hair out by the root—it's what causes the pain—and is carried out in the same way as sugaring. It's perfect if you're going long haul, as the results can last for up to two weeks.

Plucking is ideal for eyebrows and coarse hairs growing in inconspicuous places. If you want to tidy up your eyebrows, do so after a warm bath, as the steam opens up the skin's pores, making the process less painful. Use a magnifying mirror if you have one, and stretch out skin underneath the hairs with one hand, using the other to hold the tweezers and to pluck. Be wary of overplucking eyebrows, though—just follow the natural shape of your brows for a gorgeously groomed result.

Moisture injection

In hot weather, skin can easily become dehydrated, making it dry and less youthful-looking. To get it back to its plump, dewy best, you need to make sure you keep it well moisturized.

Drinking lots of water will help, as this hydrates your skin from within. And you can combat the drying effects of the sun with a good moisturizing lotion or cream. Use it as a base before you apply your sun cream; this will help it sink more easily into the skin, so you'll get a more even coverage. Look for a lotion that contains anti-aging antioxidants like vitamins A, C, and E and nourishing oils—score extra beauty gold stars if you find one with added SPF. Basic baby oil is also a great moisturizer—but don't ever be tempted to use it as a replacement for sun cream. You'll always need to apply at least an SPF15 (if you have darker skin that tans easily) or up to SPF30 (if you are fair-skinned) in order to protect yourself from the skin-damaging effects of UV rays.

When you apply your moisturizer, start from your toes and work upward toward your chest and shoulders—and don't forget your neck. Gently massage it in using a firm touch, concentrating on areas that are typically prone to dryness, such as elbows, knees, and feet. Use your usual face cream, then apply sun cream over the top. Try this nourishing aromatherapy blend.

MOISTURIZING AROMATHERAPY BLEND

This light, fragrant massage oil is suitable for all skin types.

METHOD

1 In a clean, plastic pitcher, stir the following oils so that they blend together.

$2^1/_2$ tbsp soya oil

$2^1/_2$ tbsp almond oil

4 tsp wheatgerm oil

20 drops geranium essential oil

20 drops orange essential oil

2 Decant the fully-mixed oil into a clean, sealable plastic bottle with a screw top.

3 To use, massage into the skin using long, firm, upward strokes.

Be a real smoothie

Your face needs exfoliating too, but many body scrubs are too harsh to use on the delicate skin on your face. Try this recipe for a gentle almond, honey and lemon facial scrub that can be used on even the most sensitive of skins. Ground almonds remove dead cells and smooth the skin, while honey is hydrating and lemon juice tones the pores.

1 Place two tablespoons of ground almonds in a saucer. If you are allergic to nuts, substitute fine oatmeal instead.

2 Add two tablespoons of good-quality honey and two tablespoons of lemon juice.

3 Mix all the ingredients together, then apply to the face in small circular movements, avoiding the eye area.

4 Leave on for 15 minutes, then massage into the skin once more using warm water.

5 Rinse thoroughly and finish by applying a nourishing moisturizer or serum.

Tighten and tone

Many women swear by using a toner as part of their morning and evening beauty routine for soft and glowing skin. Toning lotions are designed to get rid of traces of makeup and tone and tighten pores, making them less visible. Try this recipe for a freshening melissa herbal toning lotion. Use after cleansing, but before moisturizing:

1 Prepare a melissa infusion by putting two tablespoons of chopped fresh melissa leaves in a small heatproof bowl.

2 Pour over a cup boiling water, and let infuse for 15 minutes. Strain, then refrigerate.

3 Apply the infusion to the skin with a cotton wool pad. Your skin should feel fresh and clean.

Purify your complexion

The last thing you want to deal with while on holiday are blemishes. Suffering a break out mid-break will ruin your barefaced beach-babe look, and you won't want to spend ages back at the hotel wielding a cover-up stick, either. Help to ensure that you have a clear complexion for the duration of your holiday by putting in the groundwork before you go. This facial steam will help get rid of pore-clogging dirt and grime, and leave your skin squeaky-clean. Simply follow the directions below:

CAMOMILE & MELISSA FACIAL STEAM

Steam opens up your pores and eliminates impurities, while melissa and camomile are extremely soothing to the skin.

1 Wash and chop a handful of fresh melissa leaves and camomile flowers.

2 Pour near-boiling water into a medium-size heatproof bowl until it is half full.

3 Scatter the herbs on the surface of the water, then lean over the bowl with your face in the steam and your head under a towel. Stay under the towel for about 15 minutes, then wipe your face with a damp cloth and pat it dry.

Avocado, cypress & lavender nourishing mask

Avocado is full of vitamins A, D, and E, which nourish and protect the skin. Lemon juice and cypress oil tone the pores, and lavender acts as a soother.

1 In a small bowl, mash the flesh of half a ripe avocado.

2 Add one teaspoon of lemon juice, then two drops of cypress and three drops of lavender essential oils.

3 Apply the rich green paste all over the face, avoiding the eye area.

4 Leave on for 15 minutes, then wash off with tepid water and pat the skin dry.

Have heavenly hands

Hands that have been neglected in the beauty stakes are often the first thing to give your age away. Make sure yours are well and truly pampered, with these natural recipes.

SUGAR & LEMON EXFOLIATING SCRUB

This smells good enough to eat. Sugar granules gently exfoliate the skin while lemon tones and cleanses, and apricot oil helps soothe and nourish. This recipe should be enough to use on two pairs of hands—so you can treat a friend, too.

1 Put two tablespoons of granulated sugar in a small glass bowl.

2 Add the rind of one organic lemon and one tablespoon of lemon juice, plus two tablespoons of apricot kernel carrier oil. Stir together.

3 Apply a small amount and work gently into the hands, including all the fingers. Wipe off any excess with a damp paper towel.

YLANG-YLANG WARM OIL HAND SOAK

Ylang-ylang is a skin-conditioning essential oil that has a lovely exotic floral aroma. This recipe will make enough oil to use on two pairs of hands. You can save any leftovers for a second application if desired—simply re-warm before use.

1 Pour enough near-boiling water to half fill a medium-size heatproof bowl.

2 Pour four teaspoons of apricot kernel carrier into a smaller heatproof bowl and add four drops of ylang-ylang essential oil.

3 Stand the small dish in the larger bowl of hot water to warm the oil.

4 Once it has been heated through, lift the small dish out of the bowl and soak each hand in the warm oil for around five minutes. Wipe off any excess with a damp paper towel.

Freshen up your feet

Smelly feet are a common problem in the summer months. It happens because the sweat glands are working in overdrive to try and cool down (through sweating), but wearing shoes means the skin can't breathe properly and there is nowhere for the sweat to go. The feet become warm and moist, creating an ideal environment for bacteria to thrive, and it's this that actually produces the odor. Sticking to open-toed shoes or sandals will help keep feet fresh, but if yours are still pungent, use these freshening recipes...

OLIVE OIL & LAVENDER FOOT SCRUB

The olive oil in this recipe is supremely nourishing and great for dry skin, while the lavender helps to refresh and soothe the skin.

1 Pour six tablespoons of extra-virgin olive oil into a small bowl.

2 Add two teaspoons of fine sea salt—which makes an excellent exfoliator—and stir.

3 Add 20 drops of lavender essential oil, and stir to mix thoroughly.

4 Rest your feet on a paper towel on top of a bath towel. Then carefully apply the scrub to one foot at a time, using small circular movements all over the foot, concentrating especially on any dry areas such as heels.

5 After massaging in the scrub for 10 minutes, use the paper towel to wipe off any excess.

6 Repeat the massage with the other foot, again wiping off excess scrub at the end.

ROSEMARY HERBAL FOOT SOAK

As the rosemary leaves infuse into the liquid, they will gently deodorize and tone the skin, helping to banish odor. For an extra-softening boost, add six tablespoons of whole milk to the water.

1 Half-fill a large plastic bowl with warm water. It should be big enough to soak both your feet at once.

2 Add a handful of washed and chopped fresh rosemary leaves, and place your feet in the bowl. Add the whole milk if desired.

3 Let the feet soak for 15 minutes; if you have very dry heels, rub a pumice stone gently on the hard skin to smooth it.

4 Lift your feet out of the bowl and place onto a towel to dry thoroughly.

Relax and nourish

A leg and foot massage can be incredibly relaxing. Not only will it help to minimize stiffness after exercise, but it will also encourage toxins out of the muscles, helping them work more effectively. Use this stimulating aromatherapy blend as a massage oil to encourage detoxification.

CYPRESS, LEMON & JUNIPER AROMATHERAPY BLEND

This makes enough to use on two pairs of legs—so you can save and reuse or treat a friend. Cypress tones the circulation while lemon and juniper encourage the elimination of toxins.

1 Pour four teaspoons of sweet almond oil into a small dish.

2 Add three drops of cypress, four drops of lemon, and three drops of juniper essential oils, and stir together. Use as needed.

FOOT AND LEG MASSAGE

You need to enrol a willing friend to help you with this. Ask them to follow these directions:

1 Set up the massage with your partner lying face down on the floor on a comfortable mat or futon covered with towels. Rest her head on a pillow and keep the upper part of the body covered and warm while you work on the legs. Kneel by your partner's feet or by the calves on whichever side feels comfortable to you.

2 Stroke one teaspoon of the blend up both legs at the same time, starting from the feet and passing over the ankles, up the calves and thighs, to just below the buttocks. Spread the oil well, and repeat these strokes several times; apply more pressure up the leg and ease off as you come down.

3 Use the heels of your hands to apply slow, firm, circular pressure all over the soles of the feet and then over the calves. This soothing movement works all the main muscle groups.

4 Continue up the legs, using the heels of your hands to apply slow, firm pressure over the backs of the thighs. Be sensitive to your partner and check that the massage is comfortable for her.

5 Starting above the knees, make vertical lines of individual thumb pressure up toward the buttocks; press for a few moments, then move up a few inches and press again. Begin on the outsides of the thighs and work inward.

6 Repeat the strokes in step one, using long sweeps up the backs of both legs, with more pressure going up than coming down. Slow down the strokes and ease off to finish.

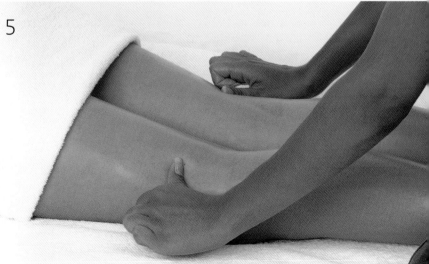

5

4

Pretty hands and feet

Well-manicured hands and feet add the finishing touch to your beach look. Well cared-for nails make you appear more polished—literally!—and a bit of color will look great in the sun. Vibrant reds, pinks, and oranges all look good in bright light, so be adventurous.

EASY MANICURE AND PEDICURE

1 Massage a blob of moisturizing lotion into your hands and wipe any excess off your nails with a tissue.

2 Trim your nails with a pair of nail scissors so that they are all the same length.

3 Get rid of any rough edges with a nail file—aim for a classic oval shape.

4 Apply a base coat of clear nail polish—this will stop the colored polish from staining them. Let dry.

5 Apply the colored polish. For a streak-free finish, start by painting a line down the center of the nail, going from the nail bed to the tip of the nail. Then add more polish in the same way either side until the whole nail is evenly covered. Let dry, then add a second coat.

6 Add a clear topcoat of varnish. It will help the color last longer and stop it from chipping. Remember to take the varnish and a nail file with you on holiday to top up the color if needed.

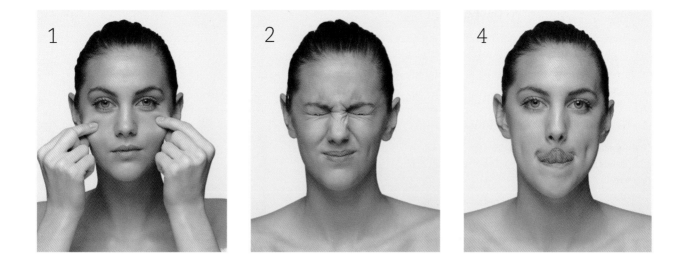

Five-minute face-lift

These simple facial exercises will help to tone and uplift the skin, giving you a younger-looking complexion in minutes. If you have never done exercises like this before, start gently and increase gradually.

For this exercise routine, pull your hair back and off your face. Your face should be cleansed and moisturized, and your hands should be dry and clean. Start slowly and gently to warm up, and relax afterward by taking a few deep breaths.

1 Using your thumb and forefinger together, pick up folds of skin all over your face, and gently squeeze, then release them. This exercise stimulates the circulation and wakes up the face. Continue for about one minute.

2 Make a really screwed-up face, hold it for three seconds, then slowly release your muscles. Repeat this exercise three times. This move tenses and relaxes all the facial muscles and works on areas that may not normally be well exercised.

3 With your mouth closed, pretend you are chewing something. Notice the direction in which you chew naturally, and do this exercise for about half a minute; then try to chew the other way. Don't overdo this movement; just chew slowly for about one minute in total. This exercise stretches the muscles of the jaw area and also the chin.

4 Stick your tongue out and try to touch the tip of your nose. Don't force this movement: go only as far as you can, then relax. This movement exercises the muscles under the chin area. Repeat three times.

5 With your lips closed, use your tongue to "brush" your teeth; this action creates a really interesting feeling, because the tongue is so sensitive. As well as increasing the production of saliva in your mouth, the movement of your tongue exercises muscles in the cheeks and chin. Continue for about one minute.

6 Rub your hands together briskly, then place them over your face and feel the warmth beneath them. Breathe deeply several times.

In-shower scalp massage

This feels heavenly and will help to stimulate the hair follicles too, so your hair grows strong and healthy.

1 Lather your hair with a nourishing shampoo, then, while the shampoo is still on your hair, place both hands on either side of your head with your fingers above your ears.

2 Apply pressure in tiny, firm, circular movements with all your fingertips, then move up slightly and repeat.

3 Keep going until you have covered your whole head—your fingers will meet in the middle of your scalp.

4 Repeat this process at least twice, and feel the energy tingle under your fingers.

Have luscious locks

The sun's rays can be incredibly drying to the hair. In order to keep your locks shiny and manageable, you need to make sure that they get enough moisture. This hot-oil hair treatment and in-shower scalp massage will work wonders.

CARDAMOM HOT OIL HAIR TREATMENT

Work this treatment into dry hair for best results.

1 Pour enough boiling water to half-fill a medium-size heatproof bowl.

2 Pour two tablespoons of jojoba carrier oil into a smaller heatproof dish. Add six drops of cardamom essential oil, and stir in.

3 Place the small dish in the medium one, resting it in the boiling water to warm the oil. Set aside for 5-10 minutes, then scoop the warm oil into your hands and work it into your dry hair and scalp.

4 When your whole head is covered, take a large piece of plastic wrap and wrap your hair up in it like a turban. Wrap a warm towel around your head to finish, then sit comfortably and relax for 15 minutes. Your scalp will start to tingle and feel very warm.

5 Unwrap your head carefully. Take some shampoo and work it straight into your hair. Don't put water on before or with the shampoo, otherwise it will be very hard to get the oil out. When you have worked up a rich lather, get in the shower and rinse it all away. When dry, it will smell very fragrant.

Stay safe in the sun

You can still enjoy some time in the glorious sunshine and stay safe from the effects of harmful UV rays at the same time. Get sun savvy with these top tips:

* Always stay out of the sun when it's at its hottest, between 11am and 3pm.
* Cover up with a long-sleeved cotton kaftan and a wide-brimmed sun hat.
* Protect your eyes with dark sunglasses—make sure that they filter out UVA-UVB rays.
* Never go out without using a sun cream with a high SPF (of at least 15), and remember to reapply often if you are dipping in and out of the water or towelling yourself dry.
* Stay well hydrated by drinking lots of still water throughout the day—aim for eight glasses, or the equivalent of $4\frac{1}{2}$ pints/two liters.
* If you want to doze on a sun bed, make sure that you are in the shade and that someone is keeping an eye out and will wake you if the sun moves round so that you are in full sun.
* Don't be fooled by cloudy weather—the sun can still be very powerful, so follow sun-safe rules all times.

Hot spot! If you do get burned, get out of the sun immediately and apply a cooling after-sun lotion. If you think you may have heatstroke, which occurs when the body is unable to control its temperature due to excessive heat, you must seek medical attention immediately (symptoms include headaches, dizziness, nausea and vomiting, muscle weakness or cramps, stomach cramps, tiredness, loss of appetite, pale skin, a weak pulse, and a high temperature).

Fake it

Sun and skincare experts agree that the only safe tan to have is one that comes out of a bottle. With skin cancer on the rise, it certainly pays to fake it. The good news is that modern formulations are really easy to apply and they create a fantastic result—it couldn't be easier to get glowing. The best thing about having a fake tan is that it makes you appear slimmer and more toned. In addition, it helps to "hide" cellulite.

As you've got four weeks to go, you should choose a formulation that develops overnight but which you can build up over time. Depending on your personal preference, you can opt for a cream/lotion, a mousse, or a clear spray—all are easy to apply.

Make sure you thoroughly moisturize your skin beforehand, as it will help you to get an even result and avoid streaking. Spend time massaging the product into your skin, and make sure you cover every inch. Apply liberally to legs, arms, chest, and shoulders, and use any excess on your hands to wipe over elbows, knees, and feet (the skin here is drier, so you'll need less product). Ask a friend to help cover your back and, when you're done, make sure you tissue off any excess product that's between your fingers and on your palms. You might want to use a separate formula on your face.

It's wise to let it dry for at least ten minutes before getting dressed, otherwise the tan may stain your clothes. Most fake tanning products take 12 hours to develop, so it's a good idea to apply it in the evening. That way, you can have a shower in the morning, which will also get rid of the distinctive smell that some products create. Build your color up over a few days or weeks until you are happy with the result. It's best to apply every other day until you're satisfied, so it's a gradual process.

While you are away on holiday, use an instant bronzer, which you can see immediately when applied to the skin. Use it to top up your color as and when you need it. For added impact, invest in a shimmering bronzing powder to highlight your cheekbones and shoulders in the evening.

Use a cooling potion

After a long hot day spent baking in the sun—while observing sensible sun-safe guidelines, of course—your skin will be in desperate need of a cooling potion. Most after-sun creams contain soothing ingredients and extracts such as shea butter and aloe vera.

Make it your mission to apply an all-over cooling body cream at the end of every day. Spend time massaging in the product, starting with your feet and working upward to your neck and face, concentrating on typically dry areas such as elbows and knees. It's a simple thing to do, but the benefits will be immediate—your complexion will be soothed and glowing. Even if you haven't been in the sun, your skin will thank you for it.

SUPER SKIN SOOTHER

Aloe vera gel is a wonderful natural product that instantly cools red, itching, or sunburned skin. The leaves of the aloe vera plant contain the juice that is made into the gel. In Jamaica, where the plant grows wild, the leaves are simply picked and the liquid applied instantly to damaged skin. It is possible to buy quality aloe vera gel from health food stores; keep refrigerated and use up according to the manufacturer's guidelines.

ORANGE FLOWER WATER

This is a by-product of the distillation process that produces orange blossom (neroli) essential oil. Exquisitely perfumed, it contains minute traces of the oil. It soothes and nourishes dry and mature skins, and also gently cleanses oily or combination skins. It is particularly refreshing to use after a deep cleansing face pack. Avoid contact with the eyes. If the product gets into the eyes, rinse well with warm water.

Four-week planner

A lot can happen in four weeks—that's just 28 days (or 672 hours, or 40,320 minutes) to a beach-beautiful new you. We've devised an easy-to-follow plan that incorporates all the fantastic elements of this book to help you feel great, and glow with health in time for your summer holiday. What more inspiration do you need to get started?

How to use the planner

It's time to put the book into action. Say goodbye to bad habits and start your journey to getting beach gorgeous right now! In the four weekly planners over the page, we've given you over 112 super ideas that'll help inspire you to get going with the plan. This section is your guide to the kind of lifestyle you should strive to achieve over the next four weeks and beyond.

How it works

The four-week planner aims to give you an idea of what you should be doing every day to bolster your beach goddess potential. The tips in the planners are there to help get you on the road to looking and feeling fantastic, with advice on being more active in your daily life, opting for healthier foods, and investing time in your looks, it's the ultimate guide to getting gorgeous. Alongside the general lifestyle tips, we recommend that you incorporate ideas from each of the other sections in this book into your daily schedule. Try one kick-start tip and a few of the exercises each morning, plus a few of pampering tips as and when you need to. Feel free to group the recipes together to make a healthy day's menu, or if you feel you're running out of new things to try, why not have a go at introducing some of your own healthy tips?

Why four weeks?

We can't promise that in four weeks time you will have dramatically transformed your looks, but you are likely to notice some truly awesome results such as weight loss, a more toned silhouette, plus glowing skin and glossy hair. We believe that four weeks is all it takes to get used to a healthier lifestyle and that if you can make it that far, you'll be much more likely to stick with it in the long run. There's no deprivation required, so the plan should be enjoyable rather than taxing. To help it go as smoothly as possible, you should plan at least one week in advance, in order to get a clear idea of the kinds of recipes and beauty treatments you will be carrying out, because you may need to go shopping for certain ingredients, or hunt down some aromatherapy oils. It also helps to have a mini run-through of the exercises so you know what you are doing and won't waste time later trying to get to grips with the directions. Well, what are you waiting for?

Troubleshooting tips

Q Help! I had a very busy and social weekend, and I've missed a day of the regime.

A Try not to panic. It isn't the end of the world if you do miss a day, although it might become a problem if it happens too frequently. If you've simply forgotten, or it has been impossible to fit everything in—if you are away on business, for example—then resolve to get straight back into the plan as soon as possible. If you know you have a particularly busy or difficult few days coming up, then try to look for ways that you can incorporate elements of the plan into your schedule. If you are eating out, simply make a healthy choice—opt for grilled fish with loads of steamed vegetables or something similar. If you can't get to the gym, photocopy the pages with exercises on and take them in your suitcase to do in your hotel room. It's easy when you know how!

Q I've tried all the exercises, but there's one I just can't seem to master.

A If, for any reason, you feel pain or discomfort, light-headed, faint, or dizzy while carrying out any of the exercises, you should stop and seek the advice of your physician as soon as possible. If you simply don't like a particular exercise, then feel free to substitute another in the book—and the same goes for recipes and tips from all the other sections.

Q I've lost faith; my motivation seems to have disappeared overnight. I'm not sure I should bother carrying on.

A Don't give up so easily! Just think of all the great benefits you'll get from sticking with the plan: you'll lose weight, feel fitter and healthier, and have glowing skin and glossy hair. People think of giving up, but if they'd carried on for a few extra days they would usually have started to see the results they dreamed of. If you've quit plans in the past, it may even be your body's own way of sabotaging your good intentions, so don't listen to it! If you find that you are really struggling, then leave one element out, such as kick-start, for a few days, and reintroduce it when you are feeling stronger and more positive. We promise it will be worth it.

Week One

	KICK-START	HEALTHY EATING	EXERCISE	PAMPERING
MONDAY	Write a list of everything that makes you feel stressed, then tear it up and throw it away	Clear your refrigerator and store cupboards of unhealthy food like chips and cookies	Take the stairs today wherever possible	Stimulate your circulation by ending your shower with a burst of cold water. It'll tighten and tone the skin
TUESDAY	Call an old friend for a chat to boost your spirits	Swap your morning coffee for herbal tea	While you're on the phone, stand, instead of sit, and you'll burn more calories	Just before bed, apply a rich moisturizer to your feet, then let it sink in overnight
WEDNESDAY	Spend an evening looking at old photographs that bring back great memories	Eat everything with chopsticks—it will slow down your eating	Go for a 30-minute walk this evening—if wet, just grab your umbrella and go	Give your nails a lick of pretty polish, p82
THURSDAY	Go to bed a half hour earlier than usual	Have a delicious smoothie for lunch today	Do squats and lunges while you watch your favorite TV program tonight	Treat yourself to an exotic body scrub (p74) or fruity shower gel, p75
FRIDAY	Get creative and start a drawing or painting	Give your skin a boost by drinking plenty of water	While at your desk, squeeze your thighs and buttocks and hold for ten seconds. Repeat for a total tone up	For silky soft tresses, sleep with a deep conditioner in your hair and rinse when you wake up
SATURDAY	Arrange some freshly cut flowers in your sitting room	Invite friends over for a healthy veggie dinner party	Join a dance class tonight—it's fun and great for burning calories	De-stress by getting your partner to give you an all-over body massage
SUNDAY	Take time out to focus on your breathing—it will calm your nerves	Give your digestive system a spring clean by eating just fruit today	Get stuck into some gardening—weeding and hoeing are great for toning arms	Beach goddess essential: de-fuzz! Shave or wax your legs, bikini line, and underarms for silky-smooth skin, p76
WEEKLY WORKOUT	Choose from one of the suggested routines: a) Spine rotation p50, Seated knee lift p49, Moving curl p54, Basic lunge p61 b) Single-leg squat p60, Leg lift p66, Inner thigh lift p69, Kneeling kick-back, p67 Repeat each routine twice			

Week Two

	KICK-START	HEALTHY EATING	EXERCISE	PAMPERING
MONDAY	Boost your brainpower by doing a crossword in the paper	Opt for raw food for lunch today—try carrot, sweet bell pepper, and cucumber sticks with bean sprouts	Borrow your neighbor's dog this evening and take it for a brisk walk	Give yourself a leg and foot massage, p81
TUESDAY	Text five friends you haven't spoken to recently	Drink ice cold water today; it will help you burn more calories	Ditch the car and carry your food shopping home tonight instead	Smother your face with a nourishing mask, p78
WEDNESDAY	Volunteer a few hours of your time to charity—it'll make you feel good inside	Chew each mouthful of food 15 times—it will help you recognize when you are full	Sing up for a local 5k run—even better if it's for charity	Book yourself in for a makeover at your local department store
THURSDAY	Banish negative thoughts for the entire day	Have a peppermint tea after every meal to aid digestion	Take up a fun new hobby such as rollerblading—anything that gets you moving	Invest in a foundation that matches your skin tone perfectly
FRIDAY	Organize a swap shop in your home and trade unwanted clothes with friends	This is your antioxidant food day; drink green tea and fill up on berries and other fresh fruits	Offer to do the afternoon coffee run at work—go to the store down the street instead of the one next door	Give yourself a face lift to knock years off your look, p83
SATURDAY	Wear bright colors today	Add some spice to your food and it will help to stimulate your metabolism	Organize a group bicycle ride to the local park	Exfoliate your skin, then apply a fake tan for a gorgeous golden glow, p86
SUNDAY	Get up a half hour earlier this morning to meditate	Steer clear of wheat today—fill up on protein and vegetables instead	Get outside and give your car a wash—really scrub that motor!	Beach goddess essential: de-fuzz! Shave or wax your legs, bikini line, and underarms for silky-smooth skin, p76
WEEKLY WORKOUT	Choose from one or two of the suggested routines: a) Spine rotation p50, Easy plank p52, Side reach p57, Double knee bends p63 b) Simple seated thigh squeeze p62, Double knee bends p63, Pillow roll p59, Kneeling kick-back p67 Repeat each routine three times			

Week Three

	KICK-START	HEALTHY EATING	EXERCISE	PAMPERING
MONDAY	Make it your mission to leave work on time today	Turn off the TV and eat at the dinner table—you'll be more aware of what you're eating	Walk over to your colleague's desk instead of e-mailing	Give your skin a wake-up call by washing in warm then cold water, p75
TUESDAY	Clear away clutter in your home—get rid of any old paperwork	Swap diet fizzy drinks for diluted natural fruit juice for the day	Do 50 sit-ups before breakfast	Apply a moisturizing aromatherapy blend to your skin, p76
WEDNESDAY	Dance around your living room to your favorite music	Use honey to sweeten your food; it's healthier than sugar lumps	Get off the bus one stop earlier today and walk the rest of the way to the office	Soak your hands in warm oil, p79
THURSDAY	Have a caffeine-free day	Chew on sugar-free gum for a short while to help stimulate your digestion	Swap watching your favorite soap for a fitness video	Massage in an exfoliating body scrub to keep skin smooth and gorgeous looking, p75
FRIDAY	Put on your best dress and highest heels and enjoy a fun (alcohol-free) night out	Have a "no dairy" day and get your calcium from leafy green veggies instead	Check out the local pool, and do 50 lengths	Book yourself in for a trim at a swanky hair salon—ask for a scalp massage for an extra boost
SATURDAY	Do a face sauna in the sink to open pores and expel toxins	Swap your chocolate bar for a low-calorie hot chocolate drink after dinner	Start a running club at work—get as many people involved as you can	Make your own soothing foot soak with warm water and fresh rosemary leaves, p80
SUNDAY	Enter the pub quiz with friends—it'll get you thinking (just stick to fizzy water)	At dinner, serve up half your usual portion size	Clean you home by vacuuming, dusting, and wiping surfaces—work the upper arms	Beach goddess essential: de-fuzz! Shave or wax your legs, bikini line and underarms for silky-smooth skin, p76
WEEKLY WORKOUT	Choose from two of the suggested routines: a) Spine rotation p50, Belly tightener p51, Basic oblique curl p55, Single-leg squat p60 b) Side reach p57, Bridge squeeze p65, Outer thigh lift p68, Simple seated thigh squeeze p62 c) Seated knee lift p49, Pillow roll p59, Leg lift p66, Double knee bends p63 Repeat each routine four times			

Week Four

	KICK-START	HEALTHY EATING	EXERCISE	PAMPERING
MONDAY	Speak to someone you've never spoken to before at work	Say no to refined sugar, suck on frozen grapes if you fancy something sweet	Wear flat shoes to work today; you'll be able to be more active	Massage in a skin-firming cream to your stomach, thighs, and arms to help tighten and tone your body
TUESDAY	Book tickets to the theater or go and see a feel-good movie	Drink water before dinner so you don't confuse dehydration with hunger pangs	Put soup cans to good use—use them as dumbbells to help tone your arms	Do an in-shower scalp massage for heavenly hair, p84
WEDNESDAY	Spend 10 minutes dry body brushing before your shower	Make breakfast your biggest meal of the day	If you can, try cycling to work today	Give yourself an at-home manicure and pedicure. Hot pink polish looks great with a tan, p82
THURSDAY	Treat yourself to a piece of jewelry or a new pair of shoes—get glamorous!	Give your hair and skin a boost by eating omega-3-rich foods such as oily fish	Book a fitness class with your friend—promise each other you'll go	Go shopping for suncream—choose a clear gel to avoid greasy marks on your bikini, p85
FRIDAY	Pick some fresh flowers for your home	Say goodbye to snacking —stick to main meals only	If you want to relax in front of the TV, keep in shape by doing jumping jacks during some of the commercial break	Prepare a cooling potion to take to the beach—aloe vera has soothing properties and can help stop you peeling, p87
SATURDAY	Massage a skin-firming cream into your stomach, thighs, and arms	Go organic and cook all your meals entirely from scratch	Check out the local park—factor in a brisk stroll or game of tennis	Look glowing and gorgeous by applying fake tan—a touch of moisturizer will help you get an even result, p86
SUNDAY	Get up early today to watch the sun rise	Turn vegan for the day—exclude animal products such as meat, cheese, and milk	Spend a half hour stretching	Beach goddess essential: de-fuzz! Shave or wax your legs, bikini line, and underarms for silky-smooth skin, p76
WEEKLY WORKOUT	Choose from two or three of the suggested routines: a) Spine rotation p50, Lower abdominal raise p53, Basic reverse curl p56, Double knee bends p63 b) Double-leg push-out p58, Pillow roll p59, Inner thigh lift p69, Kneeling kick back p67 c) Simple seated thigh squeeze p62, Moving curl p54, One-legged buttock clencher p64, Bridge squeeze p65 Repeat each routine five times			

Index